www.spytv.co.uk

Spy TV

Written and edited by David Burke

With contributions from Deirdre Devers,
Jean Lotus, Simon Davies and
Ibrahim Hasan

ISBN 1 899866 25 6

Published in 2000 by

Slab-O-Concrete Publications
PO Box 148 • Hove • BN3 3DQ • UK
mail@slab-o-concrete.demon.co.uk

Printed in England

Contents

Convenience

THE CHANCES ARE you spend a quarter of his waking life in front of a TV set, perhaps saying "it's like having someone in the room." Meanwhile, because of television, you have fewer conversations, and fewer people who know you intimately.

But a new type of television is being developed. Millions of dollars are being spent to create a device that *really* is someone in the room with you, someone who will know you intimately. Matthew Timms, head of programming at Two Way TV in London describes this digital revolution you have heard so much about:

"…somehow they feel they're sitting there, it's just them and the television – even though the reality is that it's got a wire leading straight back to somebody's computer. So it actually gets sort of interesting information back."

Timms is talking about his customers, the people who pay him money each month. Perhaps they were attracted to his company's subscriber list by its promises of Choice, Fun, Convenience, and Empowerment. Control – that's what interactive television offers. Sitting on your couch, you will soon be able to have almost any product or service you desire, delivered at the touch of a button.

But what if you prefer to monitor people in their homes, any time, day or night? What if you want to build up, over years, psychological profiles of individuals from a distance – what motivates them, what makes them anxious, what makes them jump? What if you want to use that knowledge to manipulate what they know, how they feel and, finally, what they do?

Interactive television can deliver that as well. It can provide all this control to any company or government that is able to pay the money. "We can build up profiles of people," says Two Way TV Managing Director Simon Cornwell, "based on what they say and on their actual behaviour. Eventually the product will target itself to individual customers and what one customer sees will be very different from what another customer sees."

Interactive television will be used to invade viewers' privacy. Contrary to what you might have heard, that is important, because privacy was never about information; it's about power – the individual's bargaining power with the rest of the world. If you have nothing left to hide, then your negotiating position is impossibly weak. Your free will is exposed to tampering, and you may have much to fear.

If asked, people who work in interactive television will admit that this technology creates experimental conditions in the home. The machines that control your TV set will show you something, check to see how you react, and then show you something different. That's not just convenient. It is a loop of stimulus, response and measurement as carefully designed as those boxes where rats hit buttons to get food and avoid electric shocks.

And if you want to know more about those rat boxes — what year they were first used and whose theories they were built to test — ask someone who has passed his or her Chartered Institute of Marketing exam. The people who sell it call interactive television "a convergence". And it is — of so many things: marketing, child-psychology, sociology, advertising, public relations and politics. Not to mention complex adaptive systems software.

But how will it affect you? You are about to accept a powerful new device into your home, and interact with it every day for an average of four hours, that is half the time you are not sleeping or working, for the rest of your life. What is this machine designed to do? Look inside your digital set top box, and you will see much more than a TV tuner. It is actually a computer worth hundreds of dollars. Just like a PC, it contains, or will soon contain, all these components:

- **Memory:** processes data and runs programs. As with any computer, the functionality is not built into the hardware. The box will do whatever it is told to by the software.
- **Storage:** flash ROM at the moment, but within a couple of years it will be replaced with something more powerful, perhaps a hard drive. This will allow the box to store software and data, even when turned off.
- **Modem:** or a network card, which allows data to be sent back and forth over a public network. Some boxes use a phone line. The more powerful ones use coaxial cable.

That is a lot of power. Best of all, you get it for nothing. The digital TV companies have offered to buy these computers for you. Profits crashed at Rupert Murdoch's BskyB corporation, and shareholders had their dividends frozen when the company decided to pay

£315 million to give each of its current subscribers a free box. That was just the beginning. Now it must also buy a box for every new customer. Why are they doing this? Why would somebody just give you all that hardware for nothing?

Here's a hint: you have no control over what it does. Unlike a normal PC, you have no say over the hardware or software. You can't add or take out bits and pieces, you can't start, stop, install or uninstall new programs. And, in the case of Murdoch's Sky Digital, if you choose not to plug your modem in, you'll lose your "Interactive Discount" and have to pay them up to £248. That makes interactive TV a service you pay not to have.

It is hard to find out the truth about this machine, and decide whether to accept it. The only people who know anything, and are doing all the talking, are the companies trying to sell it. And they haven't been telling the whole truth – not in their television commercials, glossy booklets or their carefully worded contracts.

So we have written this book to reveal some of the missing facts. It describes the engine of this two way television, following data "straight back to someone's computer" and then back into individual living rooms. It lays out those analytic techniques that will be used to extract "sort of interesting information" and attempts to foresee how the use of such information will change us. But *Spy TV* begins with a look at that ten feet or so between your couch and the wall where all the chairs in the room are pointing.

Revolution

IT SEEMS EVERY FIVE MINUTES someone is shouting about a new digital revolution. Interactive television does have the power to change your life, but the populist rhetoric surrounding the technology discourages anyone from asking questions. "Revolution" implies something spontaneous, that would be wrong or stupid to resist, rather than something planned and offered for consideration.

The internet was a genuine digital revolution. Ordinary people used freely available technology to break down, overnight, the two main impediments to free speech: government censorship and the high costs of distribution. College students created new ways to communicate, and new types of content so fast that the legislators and businessmen are only now catching up.

Interactive television is what those same legislators and businessmen now offer in its place. They've spent millions developing it, they're spending millions to subsidise its acceptance, and they'll spend millions more to publicise it. It's being sold as the obvious next step, finally bringing email addresses and home shopping to the many people who still don't own a keyboard. "Interactive television," said a Microsoft spokesman recently, "is the internet for the rest of us."

But this will be the second time Microsoft has tried to get rid of the internet and replace it with something it controls. In fact, interactive television could accurately be described as a "digital counter-revolution". It was designed that way by the broadcasters, advertisers and a certain computer software company, who have seen the internet threaten their entire way of doing business.

Interactive television is really just that – television. It may sound like the Internet, or a telephone service, or a bank machine, or a video game. But the business model is a carefully planned extension of what you already have. Therefore, before we say anything about interactive television, we need to examine some relevant aspects of the TV we've all had till now.

And a good place to start is the Thistle Hotel in Brighton, where a friend of mine was invited to attend the screening of a new situation comedy/drama show:

"Help evaluate TV programmes and advertising" said the

invitation, "win a free shopping basket of products!"

My friend was one of fifty lucky people selected to be the audience for some brand new television. Everyone has heard of these test groups, who make or break new programmes and feature films. She could bring other people, and we went along to wield "viewer power" over the best efforts of the entertainment industry.

The conference room was already full when we signed in and collected our free orange drink. A smiley man, the night's facilitator, clapped his hands and moved up and down the aisles, talking loudly to ladies who giggled with embarrassment. He had them point to other members of the crowd who then giggled and had to pick names out of a bag.

If you've ever been to the filming of a TV show, even a serious one, you'll always see someone like him, a floor manager, whose job it is to work the crowd. Floor managers tell you how the programme will go and what is expected from you. They tell bad jokes and then pretend to be hurt when you don't laugh. They flatter and embarrass and tease the audience into playing along with the applause sign. ("Come on! You can clap louder than THAT!")

Whether the audience likes him or hates him doesn't matter. As long as they do it together – feel the same feeling, make the same noise – get involved with the show.

Our facilitator's job was the same, except he had us fill in a questionnaire about what brands of toothpaste and deodourant we would choose if we won a free shopping basket. He then announced the big moment had come. It was time to watch the pilot episode of the TV programme. The lights came down and up came the opening music of:

PS I Love You! A light-hearted cop show about a private security firm working in glamourous Palm Springs.

BANG!

The flimsy hotel door crashed open.

"EEEEK!"

The blonde woman and her hunky lover were caught in bed by a man in a leisure suit with big black hair and a gun.

"Tony no!"

Sitting there in the folding chairs, we immediately knew something was wrong. We recognised all the actors in this TV pilot. They were familiar as victims and baddies from old Columbo episodes. The picture quality was bad and the dialogue, the costumes were all ridiculous.

"What I do with her is strictly by the book."

"Yeah, the Kama Sutra"

"Bill, get Scott on the double. This looks bad."

Then the commercials came on, and everything changed. The picture and sound were clear. The ads were modern, fast paced. It was a relief. At intermission, we filled in a second questionnaire about the pilot episode.

"I hate it"

"Stupid!"

"Very poor"

"I would watch it 0 times a week"

Everyone was laughing. It made us all feel powerful to write down our opinions and make sure this programme would never appear on our television screens at home. We felt this way even though it was obvious to most of us that the research firm didn't care about the answers. This programme was 20 years old and evaluating it was obviously not the reason we were invited to come.

Once again, we filled in a questionnaire about what items we would want if we won a shopping basket. Then we filled out a third questionnaire about our age, family situation, income and shopping habits. Then the facilitator had some older man pick a last name from the bag, and the last shopping basket was claimed by a young woman in the back row. We all gave a round of applause for the lucky winner.

I asked a woman next to me, "Why are we staying? We've all given up an evening to come here. It's clear that we're not helping choose a TV show. We're also not going to win anything. They've given the last basket away. So why are we all still here?"

"I don't know" she laughed. "Just to see what happens I guess. This is my second time."

I couldn't believe it.

"Yeah," she said. "I came to one of these last month. They showed that *PS I Love You* then too. It was a different episode though."

She must be the only person on the planet to have voluntarily watched two episodes. But there we all were, doing the same thing. We knew we'd been had, but we kept watching commercials and filling out forms.

"You're beautiful! What have you done to your hair? Soft pasta, like in Italy! So many people in business are scared to open their mouths for fear of bad breath!"

No one left. We all stayed to the end and got absolutely nothing free to take home. Two weeks later, my friend was called up and asked what advertisements she remembered. She did her best to answer truthfully.

What suckers we were!

Any of these screenings at the Thistle Hotel illustrates perfectly how the television model works:

- We thought we were there to watch a TV programme. But in fact, we were there to watch the ads.
- We thought we would get something for free. In fact, we gave up our time and effort.
- We enjoyed being with other people. But we didn't talk to each other. We just listened to the floor manager.
- We didn't enjoy the show, but we kept watching anyway, hoping something worthwhile would happen. *It never did.*

The sexiest pitch for interactive television is empowerment. It will be publicised with phrases like "What can we do for you?" and "You're in control!" But television has never been about empowering viewers. The history of TV is a series of innovations designed to get hold of people and keep them watching. All the elements of broadcasting – programmes, trailers, teasers, commercials, previews, sweeps, seasons and reruns – were developed to shape what you do with the time you are not working or sleeping. The techniques have worked so well that the average person now gives up half that time, four hours a day, to watching television.

And to see how important these techniques are, you need only look at what went wrong for British Telecom when that company failed to use them during their Ipswich Video On Demand (VOD) trials. Anyone in interactive television can tell you about this trial, it has become something of a landmark.

BT designed their VOD system much as you or I might. They bought a big server and stuffed it with every TV show or movie you could think of. By hitting the right buttons, any viewer could watch any programme or film, anytime they wanted. Louisa Riddiford is BT's business development manager for internet and multimedia services. She says people in Ipswich were keen to take part.

"I think it was the feeling of empowerment more than anything. It was fitting television very much into their lifestyle as opposed to the other way around."

That sounds ideal, doesn't it? But the trial was a failure. Viewing figures plummeted. It turns out that, given a real choice, people just don't want to watch four hours of television every day. Viewers were watching a movie here or there, and then turning their sets off again. Many were standing up off their sofas and getting out of the house. VOD trials in the United States have had similar problems.

So BT had to go back to traditional television programming. They offered small selections of programmes and, importantly, took them away again. Once BT could say the magic words "Don't miss it!", viewers glued themselves back to the screen. The "last day, everything must go" pitch is what keeps television going. And contrary to what you hear, human beings do not naturally 'veg out' for long periods. They have to be taught, trained or tricked into doing it.

"This is a service," Riddiford told a conference on interactive television, "that requires intense marketing to make people research, select programmes and then actually press the buttons. If you give people too much choice, maybe they just turn off completely."

Fitting into your lifestyle was never the idea. Television doesn't work that way. The purpose of television is to make you watch television, and here is what makes good television: It keeps you watching. It gets you hooked, gets you to cancel appointments and rush home from meetings with friends. It gets everyone in a room to stop talking and listen to what is on the screen, so they won't miss anything, especially the commercials. While he was head of interactive TV for Videotron in the UK, Andrew Curry explained that relationship, and the purpose behind it:

"If you look at commercial television, the only reason [the broadcaster] wants you to watch these programmes is so they can sell you to the advertiser. But nobody ever thinks that. Or they do think it, but they've got to the point where it's so ingrained in the culture that they don't mind it any more."

And the purpose of those advertisements is described, with similar honesty, by Pat Dade of Synergy Consulting, a database marketing firm:

"The basis of all marketing, what we're all trying to do, is change or reinforce existing behaviour"

Controlling behaviour. That is what television has always been good at, whether in the service of companies who want people to buy things, or in the service of governments who want people to give up their reproductive organs.

In New York, a private firm called Population Communications International (PCI) is paid by the US government to produce soap operas that persuade viewers to sterilise themselves. Written for broadcast in China, Pakistan, India and Brazil, these harmless bits of entertainment use what's called "the methodology", first pioneered by Mexican telenovela producer Miguel Sabido.

You introduce a positive character (sterilised, small family), a negative character (fertile, big family) and a 'transitional character' who is deciding whether or not to go for sterilisation. From there, it's simple. Good things happen to the positive character. The negative character is punished in "subtle and realistic ways". And the transitional character wavers, finally choosing sterilisation, when good things happen to him or her.

The technique doubled business at Sao Paulo's vasectomy clinics in only two months. And it can be applied to anything from new farming techniques to literacy to killing Tutsis, or whatever behaviour you're trying to reinforce.

PCI's competitor, Population Communication Services at Johns Hopkins University, recommends combining government sponsored messages with product placement. So viewers might pick up a particular laundry detergent on the way to the clinic. In America, these companies have convinced soap opera producers to change their scripts. In Britain, television drama is used to promote literacy and in Russia, the BBC is producing programmes that encourage people to start their own businesses, what it calls its "Marshall Plan for the Mind".

Not just another medium

Obviously, any means of communication can be used for propaganda. But not all of them were designed, from the beginning, with behaviour modification in mind. Criticise a form of expression, and people worry you want to censor them. Quite reasonably, people question whether criticising television is any better than burning books.

And television likes to have it both ways. It flatters itself that it is the centre of our lives, our "window on the world" that shapes our democracy. On the other hand, when faced with any criticism, TV executives throw up their hands. "Lighten up!" they protest, "TV is nothing, just a bit of harmless fun."

But some forms of expression are just not worth your time. Nobody expects you to listen to every salesman who pushes his way into your living room, and you don't have to tell every politician what you think and then listen as he pretends to agree. It just happens that television was invented for the use of salesmen and politicians. And, as with "art forms" such as snuff movies or Nazi propaganda films, maybe television is not above criticism.

The Television Model in Trouble

The old broadcast television model has come under increasing pressure in the past 20 years. Criticism of viewers and their "plug-in drug" is nothing new, but some of the long term problems that social commentators in the fifties and sixties warned us about, have, in fact, materialised and become difficult to ignore.

Sociologists are counting the minutes that parents spend talking to their kids, and the hours that "battery farm" children now spend in their rooms, instead of playing outside. Speech therapists have proved TV causes delayed acquisition of language in young children and they are now looking at a possible link to attention deficit disorder.

Robert Putnam, a professor of Politics at Harvard, wanted to know why this generation have stopped volunteering with charities, neighbourhood organisations, local sports and other groups which underpin civil society. In their place, he found only "tertiary groups", allegiances to teams or political campaigns in which none of the fans or paying members actually ever meet, let alone depend on each other. When Putnam studied possible causes, the single most important one he found was television.

Why TV is not Like Other Media

Time Waste: Unlike books, newspapers, or even films, TV demands time and attention – lots of it. Most viewers will say "I just watch a little" or "I just watch the news". But if that were true, the broadcast industry as we know it could not exist. Thousands of people's careers depend on you coming home, checking out the news headlines, and then, somehow, losing track of time until you wander off to bed.

Passivity: The way "time flies" but you're not having much fun. Unlike someone reading a book, or even listening to radio, TV viewers need no imagination. They don't get much chance or encouragement to think. And when they do try to think about what they are watching, they don't have words to take apart, attack with reason, re-arrange and put together again. Instead, a producer or director holds all the tools of lighting, actors and image. TV is essentially escapist entertainment. Even when watching something educational, the viewer's job is simply to go for the ride.

Intimacy: People are encouraged to think of TV as a friend, as their "window on the world" or their "electronic hearth" where a whole family comes together. But what an important difference! Instead of people sitting around a fire talking, the masters of escapism do all the talking and tell all the stories. Instead of learning to consider, hold and then defend opinions, children learn the all purpose conversation: "Did you see...?"

And escapism is no longer a place to visit, outside of ordinary life, where it can actually do some good. On television, in the living room, escapism is taking the place of ordinary life.

Lifestyle: Put these elements together, and it can be argued that television, used as directed, is not a medium but a lifestyle. And so many people now live this way, they cannot imagine anything different. They flick through channels and demand more and better programmes, because they have lost the ability to imagine what choices might open up if they hit that other button – the little red one marked "power".

Ownership: Speaking of power, the most important feature of television is who owns it. The ability to produce and broadcast television programmes is concentrated in the hands of a few governments and a few large corporations. With this centralisation of control, who needs to burn books?

In fact, the main problem with TV isn't what you watch. It's all the things you are not doing with those four hours every day – be a child, grow up, be an adult, raise children, be a citizen. It may not get much attention on television news programmes, but when people study these missing hours, they often ask: Is this lifestyle actually compatible with anyone's family, democracy or even their sanity?

Answering with a loud "NO!" is not as cranky as it used to be. And it is less common to hear people extol television's virtues as a great educator or meeting place of the national collective consciousness. If people do talk about the "power of television" these days, they are more likely to describe it as a time waster, a nuisance, and even a public health issue. The term "couch potato" is not as funny as it used to be.

In Britain, researchers at Bristol and Glasgow universities have found that one in five children is now overweight by the age of three. They actually consume fewer calories, but are still getting fatter. As John Reilly, a physiologist in human nutrition at Glasgow pointed out: "They are replacing natural active behaviour with inactive behaviour like watching TV."

The American Academy of Pediatrics now advise that no child under the age of two should be allowed to watch television. The way it dampens interaction between parent and baby can stunt mental, linguistic and emotional development. They have instructed their 50 thousand members take a "media inventory" of any child brought to them with attention or behavioural problems.

And a small but growing number of people have taken the next logical step and thrown out their televisions altogether. Groups like White Dot in Britain and America, TV Free America, Adbusters in Canada, and other groups in France, Spain, Australia and New Zealand have begun an organised resistance to the TV lifestyle. We run a TV Turnoff Week each April, and last year 5 million people took part.

Just as important as the mounting criticism is the competition. Service and leisure pursuits form a bigger chunk of national economies, tempting viewers away from their televisions and even out of their houses. Sometimes they help revive the community TV has weakened, sometimes they don't, but they have caused something of a panic among broadcast professionals, and talk of a "battle for eyeballs" or "attention share".

The obvious example is the internet, which took everyone by surprise in the early 90s. Obviously, no one who criticises television can unreservedly embrace the internet. One cathode ray tube can be as bad as another, and there are many users wasting their lives in chat rooms who should be out chatting with real people in their street or local bar. But the internet has, to some extent, managed to threaten television. It has put a glossy new front end on the old idea of human contact, and made people wonder why they should have to spend so much time watching commercials. It reminds them that they can do better than TV's lifestyle of risk-free entertainment.

Put together the criticism, the activism, the competition from new media, and a general perception that television is old technology, an un-exciting "default" activity, and you get some very bad news for broadcasters.

Viewing figures are in decline, not by much, but enough that the American Broadcast Company launched a $43 million campaign titled "TV is Good!", with T-shirts, mouse mats and billboards proclaiming "Thank you for watching television!" They ran focus groups and surveys to find out what would make people love their tellies again.

But even the people still watching have happily sabotaged the way TV works. With the invention of the remote control and the VCR, viewers can now mute, skip over and run away from commercials. In the broadcast and advertising trade press, you will see headlines such as "The Viewer Has Escaped".

Roger Randall, interactive account manager with Agency.com, whose team designs web sites and interactive television, describes the death of the 30 second commercial:

"Ad-avoidance rates are just increasing phenomenally, so the efficiency of the ads in decreasing, while the price is increasing… People just don't want advertising. We will see a shift away from traditional advertising in five years."

Internet users can install software on their computers which filters out ads. Broadcasters' mouths went dry when they considered what this software could do to a television. They knew they had to do something.

How the Internet Challenges Television

Open access: Like the cheap, hand printed leaflets of the 18th century, the internet has given anyone with an opinion or a story their chance to be heard. High distribution costs no longer stack the deck against a single author or small group.

Less Censorship: The structure of the internet was originally designed by the US military to withstand nuclear attack by operating without any central control. Governments have had a difficult time trying to limit access to such a system, and have sometimes just given up.

No Programming: Unlike a TV viewer, an internet user logs on, gets what he or she wants and leaves. The user is not tied to a schedule. So, like the failed VOD trials, the internet fits into a small part of a busy person's life. This arrangement is sometimes referred to as "pull technology", and people like it. Advertisers are less happy.

E-Commerce: The internet has the potential to break open national economies, providing small businesses with the same sales and distribution network as huge multinational corporations.

Text Based: Even with better and better pictures, and the advent of sound files, animation and mini-cams, the internet has revived popular excitement about reading and writing. Just when we were told they were obsolete, we can again feel the power and living importance of words.

Communication: If you want to exchange messages with people all over the world, you have to have something to say. You have to have a personality robust and resourceful enough to reach out to them. You have to care enough about subjects to converse about them. TV has always shielded us from those requirements. The internet challenged its users to rediscover them.

This is real interaction, not just pushing buttons, but using the buttons to meet human beings. And it makes television look bad.

Saving Television

The television industry's response to the internet has been predictable.

First, convergence: they spoke about the need for investment in the internet, to clean it up, weed out the rogue elements, improve the picture quality and standardise the e-commerce. In other words, make it fit the television model. This did not work. The internet proved too big to tame.

Second, subversion: they bought, and continue to buy up, the internet portals, those search engines and home pages where people go first. These immediately become more TV-like and, as much as possible, promote the kind of leisure "surfing" that fits in with television. The portals now promote television brands and programmes using the familiar words "Tonight only!" or "Don't miss it!". This action is largely defensive. What cannot be bought or controlled can at least be slowed or pushed off course.

Third, replacement: digital interactive television is meant to satiate viewers' desire to join the digital age, while reassuring them that there is nothing new at all – just better commercials. As Howard Hughes, NTL's Interactive Advertising Manager admits:

"The endgame is to create a more profitable platform than the internet"

It keeps only the bits of the internet it can use, while shutting out any elements that constitute a threat to the old business model.

A Quick Technical Overview

Interactive TV is not new. Competition from the internet just gave a final push, and some useful software, to a number of technologies that were, to be honest, not doing very well.

In the 70s Warner Brothers tested some Video On Demand services. Nobody liked them. Later, in Florida, somebody tried to rig up a bunch of computers to act like an all singing, all dancing, home shopping, video demanding service. No one used it. Until now, it has been the modest, less expensive interactive services that have managed to get past the pilot stage.

The simplest is Teletext, which puts words into a tiny, unused portion of the TV signal. It's slow and ugly. But you can push buttons and get some information. That's kind of interactive.

Quicker and better looking is the system used by ACTV in New York. The broadcaster sends out a bunch of TV channels, at the same time, to ordinary cable boxes. A user can then jump between them. For instance, in Canada, Videotron offered an interactive blackjack game. If you chose to take a card, by hitting the blue button, your TV changed over to the channel showing a woman give you a card. If you chose to stay with what you had, by hitting the red button, the TV changed to another channel, showing her not give you a card. If you won, she would say "Good job!", on the other channel, the same woman would say "Too bad!"

But she didn't really care. This type of system has no return path, so the broadcaster is unable to receive any information from you. It has run for a while now, especially in the US, and increased viewer involvement with programmes and advertising. But those little buttons have, literally, nowhere to go.

So the obvious next step is to connect the TV set to the telephone. Two Way TV in Britain sends out game shows over cable, with which viewers can play along. The set top box returns viewer commands over a telephone connection. In the United States, a service called Wink works in a similar way.

But all these systems are analogue, like ordinary TV. The bandwidth is small, and a service which requires numerous channels broadcasting at once becomes expensive. Something like Video On Demand would require every programme offered to be running at all times, which is not practical.

What has now given interactive TV a real chance is digital broadcasting. Ones and zeros are replacing wave shapes and, in the air, far more information fits into the same electromagnetic frequency. The increased bandwidth allows hundreds more channels to be aired. And through cables, digital signals need not be broadcast at all. Instead, content can be sent, like web pages, to only the individual televisions that request it.

A digital interactive television will be able to do some or all of the following things:

- Broadcast content
- Address content to individual sets
- Customise content on the fly
- Send video on demand
- Receive information from the viewer's set

What is actually offered to you in your home depends on your television provider, and, to some extent, on where you live.

Europe already has a number of digital interactive services, particularly Canal Plus, which is based in France. But these have been modest in ambition, with Canal's "Shopping Mall" making only a couple of hundred sales a day. Asia is predicted to lead an explosion in demand for digital set top boxes, but probably not until standards are set and large amounts of interactive TV content are available. It is the companies now starting services in Britain and the United States that will set those standards and push the technology world-wide.

Britain is committed to turning off all analogue television in the next ten years. So every single TV in Britain has to go digital. Every provider of digital television is also offering interactive services this year or next. After a short price war, the digital set top boxes for all digital providers are now being given away free. And these boxes include features not yet available in other countries, including the use of microchip smart cards.

Much of the country's famous, and infamous, national press is owned by News International, Rupert Murdoch's company which also owns Sky and a large share of British Interactive Broadcasting. Meanwhile, Britain's cable television companies have consolidated down to two, both receiving investment from Microsoft. Within the decade, Britain's interactive market may host a spectacular battle between two of the world's largest and most aggressive media players: Rupert Murdoch and Bill Gates.

Throw in the BBC, with its reputation and experience of broadcasting to a world-wide audience, and it becomes clear that what techniques are deployed in the UK will soon gather momentum elsewhere.

The elsewhere that needs momentum is, of course, the United States, where interactive services have popped up all over. But none of them has had huge success, and most viewers have never heard of them. Here the internet has enjoyed greater penetration into homes, and a looser structure exists between companies who make television and the many companies who send it into homes. When Americans talk about digital television, they usually mean High Definition Television (HDTV), which the American networks used to convince Congress they needed ownership of all the nation's digital broadcasting bandwidth, free of charge.

Only now are those broadcasters willing to admit they don't need or want HDTV. It doesn't bring them additional revenue, like the home shopping and banking they could run through interactive TV. And viewers, who have not been threatened with any discontinuation of their analogue service, have been turned off by the high prices of HDTV sets, which sell for more than $1000. Interactive TV in America has had a low profile, and no one seriously promoting it.

However, the American situation is about to change. The country's extensive cable networks are about to go digital, making interactive TV more powerful and attractive. The big players in computers and television have begun releasing beta versions of new software. And while America Online is launching something called AOL-TV, Microsoft and Oracle are each promoting their own interactive programming environments.

Microsoft is in the process of reworking the marketing of its WebTV product. Instead of selling it as a way to access the internet, it will now be touted as a way to get "Enhanced Television". A trade organisation called the Advanced Television Forum is gathering powerful members to set standards and evangelise the concept, while Microsoft's website offers television networks a step-by-step guide to building their own interactive service using set top boxes that run Windows.

In the early 90s, computer companies, telephone companies and cable service providers all bought each other's stock. Now we will learn what they did with it.

What happens in Britain and America in the next year will set off a chain reaction in English speaking countries, followed by the rest of the world. Interactive television will become the norm everywhere because it is too profitable not to develop and, with the death of the 30-second spot, broadcasters don't have much choice.

The Fugitive Consumer

And what of the escaped viewer? Will he stay very long or very far out of the marketing man's reach? What're you kidding? Unlike the internet, which was pioneered by all sorts of people for many different reasons, interactive television has been built, at great cost, for a single purpose. As P&G CEO Edwin Artzt put it: "We may not get another opportunity like this in our lifetime.

Let's grab all this new technology in our teeth and turn it into a bonanza for advertising!"

The new media that threatened television's old revenue streams have also created new ones. Video games and the internet offer two important sets of techniques to the interactive TV bonanza – one captures the viewer again, more tightly than before; the other follows him when he leaves, wherever he goes, and eventually leads him wherever the marketer says.

The design of video games leads the innovation of a new man-machine interaction. Done well, it marries a computer's ability to play with a human's, so that, while the microprocessor and the video screen do some of the work, their ability to mimic human situations and trigger human responses does the rest. A good video game designer knows more about human emotions and response than he does about programming languages. And his or her reward is a new area of access to what the player thinks and feels.

Daniel Bobruff is the managing director of Microtime Media and pioneered the use of product placement in children's video games. For as many hours as a child plays one of Microtime's games, he or she is actually inside a commercial, taking it in.

"I don't think broadcasters want to see consumer escape because they're too scared," he says, "They don't think they'll be able to trap him again. Whereas I actually welcome it. I'm quite happy for it and ready for it… We are using a new set of rules to define the way in which a commercial presence within interactive media is done."

He makes it clear who he thinks should be in control of this digital revolution.

"It should not be a question of advertisers waiting to pick off the opportunities once they are there. Advertisers should be involved in shaping the new environment."

Bobruff's challenge to advertisers has been heard. Interactive TV will use the video game techniques he's invented in every home, every time you turn it on.

Unilever, makers of Dove Soap, have tested an interactive commercial called "Dove Cove". As Phil Swain, head of Business Development at the Consumer Media division of Cable and Wireless describes it "viewers can move from one healthful space to another, like a health club, and just be in that sanctuary". Once in that space, says Swain, viewers "get encapsulated in the brand".

This is the new advertising: You look, you listen, you push the buttons and make the noises and, just like any video game, pretty soon you've learned to do it in your sleep. It's the neuro–muscular version of an advertising jingle you can't get out of your head. Kids will love it.

Everything on interactive TV will be designed to get you involved like this, for as many hours as possible, and advertising will become indistinguishable from other programming. Microsoft, for example, has finished an interactive prototype of Baywatch which

The Fabulous Features of Interactive TV

Limited Access: The people who make and control interactive television are broadcasters. No one has any intention of opening the airwaves to everyone and every message, the way the internet does now. And in America, the great bandwidth give-away has made sure that chance has been lost forever.

In the UK, most interactive TV viewers will not even be given access to the internet, and will have to settle for what is called a "walled garden" of interactive content from their service provider.

Censorship: Believe it or not, this is a selling point. For all the commercialism and violence on TV, interactive television providers still hope that viewers will be more nervous about the internet. As argued by Casper Bowden, director of the Foundation for Information Policy Research (FIPR), "There is a clear corporatist interest in demonising the Net." Tight control over content, exercised by a few large companies, is meant to reassure people who have heard that cyberspace is nothing but a rendezvous for paedophiles and bomb makers.

Push Technology: Web browsers now come with a button at the top marked "Channels". Hit it, and you'll most likely see names like "ABC", "CNN", or "BBC". These links use "push" technology, which was hailed as the next big thing on the internet. Instead of going out and finding what they wanted to see or read, content providers would constantly update data on users' machines. Its use on the internet has been limited, but the push concept is crucial to interactive television. If a large choice of programmes increases the risk that users will turn off their sets altogether, it is necessary to limit that choice again – package it dynamically into something fleeting and exciting. Television depends on the "big event". Something has to get viewers staying in to see it.

combines product placement with online shopping. When characters on the show win a Princess Cruise Lines holiday, viewers can hit a button and try to win their own.

How's this for convergence? Expect your email to include links to commercials featuring characters from your favourite TV shows which all include product placement and one-touch online purchasing, linked to hour-long infommercials that look and feel like your favourite video games which contain branding and more commercials. And so on.

That something is the Electronic Programme Guide (EPG) – the on-screen television listing which allows users to choose programmes. It's like a web browser, except it doesn't go where you tell it to go. It only goes to the places it offers, and is designed to nudge viewers into profitable directions.

Ashley Highfield, vice-president of Flextech, a company that develops EPGs, told Broadcast magazine: "If you have control of the EPG, then you have control of the subscribers and you can push them where you want them to go."

E-Commerce: If e-commerce on the internet threatened to open up competition, so that every tiny business had the ability to trade with the world, interactive television closes that threat back up.

As with commercials on ordinary TV, e-commerce on your television will be costly and tightly controlled. Participation will be limited to the same kinds of companies who advertise on television at the moment. And the people buying things won't be doing research, like they do on the internet now. They'll be vegging out, hitting the Buy Now button with glazed eyes and moist chins.

Picture Based: Interactive TV's big advantage over the internet is its bandwidth. Rather than a few still pictures and some crude video, interactive television delivers all the flashing, sexy, moving images that a viewer could ever hope to sit and stare at for hours.

Entertainment: Interactive TV is not about communication. It may offer email, but the primary goal is escapism, just like ordinary TV. And the only interaction most viewers will have is have is with the software. Like a video game, or a coin operated gambling machine, an interactive TV is designed to get you deeply involved with a machine.

This is the broadcasters' idea of interaction. Yes, you'll get your email, but the relationship they really want you to enter is not one with other people. It's a lasting friendship with soap packaging and insurance company mascots. TV will project your deepest desires onto beer bottles and candy bars. It is what television always has been – interaction with brands.

And those brands are no longer just pretty logos or memorable characters. They are about to come into your home as sentient beings, watching you as you relax, and making decisions about what to do with you next. If video games have taught television how to bond tightly to viewers, the internet has shown how to extend that bond all the way back to a central computer. The anti-advertising group Adbusters have a good slogan about television: "the product is you". Well, someone has decided it's time for a little stock control.

The New Television Business Model

If you live in St. Louis, you can sign up for something called InTouch television. Their website (www.intouch.com) tells you all the advantages:

- Be an active participant!
- Order a pizza with the touch of a button!
- Play along with game shows or participate in a news poll!
- Respond to trivia questions during programs!

InTouch is a brand name for the interactive service installed by Koplar Interactive Systems International, using their exclusive Veil II technology. Their website, at www.k-isi.com, tells local cable companies all the advantages:

- See and track the actual results of your advertising
- Accurately track your content and its impact on viewers
- Know where a spot aired, at what time, for how long, and who watched
- Pinpoint your message to a specific demographic, geographic, individual zip code or household

What is this second website saying? It seems that for every service that is offered to you, the paying viewers, there are other services offered only to the people behind your TV screen. While the TV providers will spend millions of dollars this year promoting the fun and convenience of interactive games and gadgets, those same companies will be reading reports like the one written by Neal Murray, marketing director of The Database Group in Bristol.

His report, The March of Digital Interactive TV and the Emerging Science of Telegraphics, was a wake up call to advertisers and direct marketers, explaining that the real "golden opportunity" of interactive TV is the chance to sit on the couch with people, in their own homes, and note what they do:

"The most important data" he wrote "which the interactive TV broadcaster can monitor and use to build new targeting systems, is information on what each household watches. This data offers properties which no other available dataset can provide."

His words were reprinted widely in the trade press, but few ordinary viewers have any idea that interactive television will work this way. Unless they paid the £1195 to get in, ordinary viewers could not attend the two day conference in London this year, at which executives from Microsoft, British Airways, Grey Advertising, Saatchi and Saatchi and other companies talked over what to do with all the information they will be getting.

At the conference, Interactive TV Advertising: Revolutionising the Advertising Industry, the TV providers and their consultants were saying very different things from what they've been telling the general public about fun and convenience. Phil Swain, head of Business Development at the Consumer Media division of Cable and Wireless was there. He is enthusiastic about what his company really sells:

"Changing channels, selecting certain programmes, viewing habits, browsing through interactive sites, purchasing habits, all that kind of stuff we can track. Every click, we can track. We will be recording that information."

Every digital set top box in your house will be uniquely identified. It's modem will give your television set what is called a return path, sending data back to the company who gave you the box. This data will be generated as you interact with a rich environment of programmes, services and games.

What do you watch? How long do you watch? Do you sit through commercials or change the channel? What would make you watch all night? What would make you click a button or buy something? Who is in the room with you? When do you go away on vacation? How do you win or lose at strategy games? What character would you choose to be in a video fantasy game?

"In the course of navigating around the system, viewers reveal a great deal about themselves," says Nick Bryant of BiB. "You're talking a couple of Cray supercomputers just to deal with the amount of information that comes back."

This is television's new business model – a powerful extension of its mission to keep you watching and influence your behaviour. The most important feature of digital interactive TV is not that you can push different buttons, but that any button you push can be recorded. Even if you never "play along" with what is on the screen, just turning it on and changing the channels will produce meaningful data that somebody can use.

Talk about empowerment! It is often said that "information is power", and "information is the new economy". Well, interactive TV is going to be taking, using and selling yours.

Military Surveillance for the Rest of Us

As you move through the peaceful sanctuary of "Dove Cove", you are being followed. Every "healthful space" you visit is recorded for the manufacturer, Unilever.

Of course, computers have been doing this for decades. In the 1960s Nielsen audits gathered 8 million bits of information about what was produced. In the 1970s, warehouse data was used to compile 130 million bits of data about what was sold to retailers. In the 1980s, store scanner data was used to amass 200,000 million bits of data about what people bought. And, according to Andersen Consulting, the 1990s have seen the focus move closer, to the household level. Systems that hold your address now produce 300 million million bits of information.

As Member of Parliament Bruce George told *The Big Issue* magazine, "Only 10 years ago, all this knowledge was only in the possession of a handful of people like the CIA. Now these companies can get hold of this information in seconds, when before it would have taken a thousand lifetimes."

But we are all about to take the next step, as these computers move from observing households to observing individuals. Taken to this smallest unit, the use of such data becomes one to one marketing, a philosophy of "relationship marketing" that has exploded in popularity. Mark Albert is the director of business development at Alto, a database consultancy helping one of the interactive TV providers do direct marketing:

"It's about creating as much information about each consumer as you possibly can," he says, "and using that in the most expedient manner to get your product to them and them using your product in specific consumer segments, ideally going to the segment of one".

Just when new media is breaking down the mass audience, one to one marketing gives companies hope that such dismemberment will be a good thing. Instead of buying a million ads and showing them to everybody, companies will now run, say, ten thousand ads and show them to the people most likely to buy. The emphasis of any advertising or public relations campaign has shifted from size to accuracy. And for this reason, every sale, complaint or phone call is recorded. Nothing is thrown away in the hope that a company can discover what customers really want, or can be made to want.

The gurus of one to one marketing, Don Peppers and Martha Rogers call this a Learning Relationship. According to them, instead of selling one product at a time to as many customers as possible in a particular sales period, the one to one marketer uses customer databases and interactive communications to sell one customer at a time as many products and services as possible, over that customer's entire lifetime.

What really boosted excitement in one to one marketing was the internet, where the right combination of online forms, cookies and software can makes information capture effortless. The data is used to control what happens when each person visits.

And that data is not limited to the customer's dealings with the one company. Because the same internet sits between all purchases anywhere, along with all the other online behaviour – browsing, searching, chat etc. – the information available about an individual consumer can be broadened to give a more complete picture. The aim is to discover not just what a person buys, but why he buys it.

As Michael Thiemann of Aptex Software told *Wired* magazine about his SelectCast ad-targeting engine: "We can predict straight or gay, whether you like sports, and a hundred other things. You could be white, male, age 40, but you act like a 16 year old Hispanic woman."

Privacy groups are fighting to hold back these companies, as they have Intel's plan to uniquely identify each Pentium III microprocessor, a plan they call "Big Brother Inside".

But what companies know about internet users is nothing compared to what television providers will know about their customers. Instead of a decentralised communications technology, throwing up legal and political battles as it is put to new uses, the "internet for the rest of us" is a sales machine, designed, from the start, to gather information on users.

It seems the night watching commercials at the Thistle Hotel also demonstrated how television will work in the future:

- The floor manager 'interacted' with us in ways designed to keep us sitting there, playing along while his company obtained information from us.
- The questionnaires were designed to make us feel powerful; we thought we were taking a stand. But no one actually read the answers we cared about. It made no difference to them what we thought of *PS I Love You*. That was just a way to make us feel good about giving them other information that they *did* care about.
- Here is a question that was important to them: could we remember the ads long after that night? Had the evening been able to influence our ordinary lives?

Television has always told viewers that their ordinary lives were boring compared to the glamourous world of TV. And after dropping friends and activities to watch their favourite shows, most viewers have come to believe it. That's why they ask non-viewers "What do you DO if you don't watch TV?" But broadcasters and advertisers know the truth, that the hours and days of a viewer's ordinary life are all there is. They are the prize; they are what the game is all about.

Interactive TV is just the latest "virtual" life on offer in exchange for the only real life you will ever have. Similarly, the people providing it plan to make large sums of money selling information about you. They won't just get it for free, you will be paying them to take it.

The Hardware

The simplest and most powerful is cable. It puts a television into real time, two-way, 24 hour a day communication with a head office computer. In the United States, cable is king – 70% of homes are connected. This vast infrastructure is why, even though America lags behind Europe in take-up of digital interactive TV, it will catch up quickly. In Britain, the cable companies have had difficulty building a customer base. Firstly, the free television is simply much better. But most of the people who do pay for television subscribe to Rupert Murdoch's Sky TV, a satellite television company.

The technology of satellite interactive television is limited. The TV receives signals from a dish, but can only send them back by making a telephone call. If you buy something online, you will see your TV set make a phone call. If the head office wants to gather information about you, the set top box will have to make its own phone call. So it must have enough storage to save transaction information over the course of the day.

Another form of digital interactive is Microsoft's WebTV, which puts internet content onto a TV screen, where it may or may not be linked to what is broadcast. What many users don't know is that WebTV captures data about what they watch, and where they surf. At night, the information is quietly sent to Microsoft. This year, Tele-Communications Inc. and other cable operators will install more than 5 million cable set top boxes built to run WebTV.

"I don't think people understand the extent of this," said Tom Rheinlander, an analyst at Forrester Research Inc. told Inter@ctive Week Online, "It's recording everything they do. This is like having a video camera on them 24 hours a day."

A fourth architecture worth mentioning is that of K-ISI's InTouch service. Using their "Veil II" technology, this company hides signals in ordinary analogue television, which are then picked up by a small box at the back of the TV set. The small box sends instructions to a special cordless telephone that customers must install. This arrangement is similar to the one used by the Barney, and soon Teletubbies, ActiMates dolls, which sit next to children and interact with their respective TV programmes.

The really important upgrades will replace software. All the interactive televisions described above can download new programmed instructions from their head office at any time, without any effort, or permission from the owner. So the box you own next week may be doing entirely different things from the one you buy today.

Choice

There's this family who appear in any article about interactive television.

When Sky Digital was launched in Britain, *The Times* gave away a magazine supplement featuring this family's busy day: "Mom wants to check the train schedules... click!", "Dad wants to buy a new lawn mower... click!"

In *The Telegraph*, this family were called the Viewers. Mr. and Mrs. Viewer had just bought a huge black television called "the Millennium", and rearranged their home to make room for it. Then they sat back and were "pleasantly surprised" at a bunch of things they could buy. They would never have to leave their house again.

Oh, what a happy little 1950s kind of family are the Viewers. How cosy their little home, neatly packed with As-Seen-On-TV impulse purchases and From-The-Comfort-of-Your-Own-Living-Room services. It only seems right that if we're going to write a book about interactive TV, we should have our own happy family:

Even before their new Telescreen® set-top box arrived, The SpyTV company knew a great deal about Winston and Julia Smith. They had filled out a lengthy questionnaire in the shop, which had been attached to their warranty, and seemed important. It asked them about their:

Address
Occupation
Family members
Ages
Income
Ownership of various things
Purchases on the internet
Purchases from TV ads

Now, on Tuesday the 14th, at 3:47pm and 28 seconds, Winston turns on his new Telescreen® TV for the first time. It knows what he has done! "Hello! Welcome to SpyTV!" says the screen. "Would you like to customise your SpyGuide Now?" Winston is pleasantly surprised.

To understand what an interactive TV will do in your home, it helps to know a little about computer programming. The set top box you buy will use software, probably written in an object oriented, event driven language. Let's imagine briefly what Winston's TV television is doing.

Every time Winston clicks a button on his remote, it fires a software trigger called an event. It is a chance to run some computer code. So, for instance, if you wrote some code that caused the television to beep, and attached it to the ButtonDown event, then every time Winston hit a button the television would beep.

There are many kinds of events, and any of them can hold any amount of code. But the code running on interactive television always does one of three things:

- It sends you the television and services you ask for.
- It gathers and stores information about you.
- It uses the information for some purpose.

You will hear plenty of talk about that first type of code, the fabulous programmes you can watch, and games you can play. So we won't be discussing it here. Instead, this chapter and the next will concentrate on the functions of interactive television that no one is telling you about – how it gathers and uses your personal information.

Let's look at the code triggered by events on Winston's TV. He turns it on at 3:27 and 48 seconds, by hitting the Power button. An event on that button adds a record to a Log table in the database, recording what button Winston pushed and when. This raw data is most important. By saving every click and adjustment, it is possible to work out exactly what Winston watched and typed during the evening – his viewing behaviour. The log of his activity can then be saved until someone thinks of a new way to analyse it.

But even now there are small calculations to make and other tables to fill. And that work can be spread around – some of it done on the client, some on the server, some in real time, and some at the end of each day, or week.

For instance, hitting the power button turns on the TV, so a SessionStart event is fired and a record is added to another table in the database called ActiveSessions. Since it is Winston's first time, let's call this session ID number 0000000001.

This session ID number, plus Winston's Box ID number can be added to new records in a Programmes Watched table, which grows as the night goes on. Every programme or commercial is split into scenes, each with its own Scene ID, and this number is kept on the set top box, changing as the scenes progress. Whenever Winston changes the channel, a ChannelHop event fires, closing the current record of the Programmes Watched table after inserting a Scene ID and the Stopped Watching time. The ChannelHop event then opens a new record in the Programmes Watched table for whatever Winston sees next.

When he finally goes to bed, a SessionEnd event retrieves Winston's record in the ActiveSessions table and a SessionStop time is added. The SessionEnd event also runs through a collection of ad hoc programs, little bits and pieces that have been downloaded from SpyTV headquarters just for Winston. There can be any amount of code and any number of tables. As time goes by, every event will fire more code, filling more tables for anyone who wants to know about Winston and his family.

Of course, we had to make up this example of data capture. What your interactive television provider does with its observations of you is a company secret, protected by copyright laws and confidentiality agreements. Neither we, nor you, have access to that information. But such a system is the minimum required for the analysis broadcasters have already told us they plan to do. What you have been reading here is just the beginning.

"There is no limit to this technology," says Howard Hughes of NTL, "The limit is only as far as the mind can imagine."

As Spy TV is launched, most of the software running is operational, that is, it provides the functionality that viewers like Winston think they are paying for. But as time goes on, the majority of software will become analytical, that is, it provides functionality to people who wish to know things about Winston, or change what he does.

"The cable companies," predicts Neal Muranyi of the Database Group, "will ultimately become big power brokers of information,"

Who are these people who buy Winston's personal information? Some of them will work for manufacturers, their advertising agencies

Raw Data Your Interactive TV Will Collect

Welcome Pack Questionnaire: As they often include "warranty cards", people feel obliged to answer a long list of questions unrelated to the product, including income, profession, number of children, newspapers taken, other products owned, and so on.

On-Off Times: When? How often?

Shows Watched: Which were seen in part, which seen from start to finish? What tiny bits of shows were seen as the viewer flicked through channels, and how long did the viewer remain? It is possible to ad coding to a show as it runs, and answer such questions as what was happening on the screen just before the viewer turned the channel?

Electronic Programme Guide (EPG): What pages and lists of programmes were viewed? How is the guide used?

Commercials Watched: Which viewed to completion, which viewed in part, time spent

Commercials Clicked: Whenever the viewer hit a "tell me more" icon, time spent reading or watching the further information. Other clicks to other information screens.

Commercial Purchases: Which ads persuaded a viewer to click on an order form, which ads lead all the way to an online sale.

Services Used: Which services, such as email, diary, chat, weather, stock market quotes, shopping, viewing planner, child viewing filter etc. How often used, every keystroke typed in to any of the services.

Online Shopping: Where viewer browsed, where viewer almost bought or requested more information, when and what was bought.

Forms and Surveys: Viewer requests for information, pop-quizzes, viewer opinion polls, electronic programme guide preferences, programme suggestion forms, game or activity entry forms.

Games and activities: Every click to move characters in games of hand-eye co-ordination, scores, preferences and all choices or actions in games of fantasy and strategy.

and public relations firms. Others will work for governments or international bodies. Some will work for non-profit organisations, individuals, or just the highest bidder. Let's call these outside people, whom Winston and Julia will never meet, the Watchers.

Maybe you don't think the buttons you click when you watch TV could tell anybody very much. But the Watchers will be pleasantly surprised at the way viewer behaviour helps them do other, more sophisticated, kinds of analysis. With the exception of telegraphics, all the methods listed below have been used for years. Each has its specialists. Some have trade journals and business conferences. They only wait for better access to you and your family.

Click! Some company wants to know what you buy... click! Another wants to exploit a relationship with your child... click! A pressure group, funded by a trade organisation, wants to know your politics... click!

Telegraphics

It's all about choice. All the choices a viewer makes, from solemn decisions to fleeting impulses, reveal things about him that can be used, if you know how to look at them the right way. The first kind of analysis then is viewing analysis, what Neal Muranyi called "telegraphics".

It will be easy for broadcasters to create the following reports about viewers of interactive television:

- Viewing hours over week
- Channel choice over week
- Loyalty to shows
- Who watches a certain show or shows, in order by wealth of neighbourhood
- Advertisements missed or seen
- Viewer restlessness by type of programme
- Viewer restlessness by type of advertisement
- Response to big events

These reports are simple but powerful. They describe behaviours in each household that broadcasters and advertisers have long dreamt of knowing. How many people are watching a car programme, for how long, and how many of them live in wealthy neighbourhoods?

Who Are The Watchers?

Advertisers • Marketers • Public relations firms • Government agencies • Police • Manufacturers • Lifestyle data companies Private investigation services • Your employer • The highest bidder

Who are they? What are their addresses? It has been shown that the more involved viewers are in what they watch, the more likely they are to accept advertising messages. Interactive TV has been shown to increase involvement, and can also be used to measure it in clicks and keystrokes.

Telegraphics is vital in any strategy to keep you in front of the screen. How do you and your family use television? What content on TV, and situations outside, combine to make you watch more? When do you turn it off altogether? How can you be stopped from doing this?

But beyond selling air time, television providers are now in the business of selling data or the use of data. And their data customers, the Watchers, will be asking other questions which spring from the types of analysis described below. To them, viewing and online buying are behaviours to study, and telegraphics will put that viewing data into a form they can use. What they get will be more varied and meaningful than just changing channels. Telegraphic analysis will also tell advertisers which viewers clicked on what ads or took a peek where, how long they peeked, who played a game, how they played etc.

Like Dove Cove, programmes can also be specially produced to elicit information from viewers. Two Way TV has run many online surveys, and Matthew Timms remembers he was surprised at the way viewers loved to answer even personal questions. Here he explains that viewers need not know they are providing information, because the questions are just part of the fun.

"If it's a programme with the interactivity sort of inherent in it, then that's easy because you just insert questions which give you the information that you require as part of the entertainment. You have to take a reasonably moral approach to it (laughter)."

Ha ha ha! With the average viewing time for most people in Britain or America approaching four hours a day, there has never been so much data to study. In fact, so much and so many different

37

viewing behaviours will be recorded that humans will not have time to study them all. However, as will be shown, computers have now learned to do their own studies, and ask their own questions.

Demographics

The first type of consumer modelling is based on your address. Just your TV subscription form brings with it a large amount of information that is regularly kept about neighbourhoods, streets and even the houses where people live. It is enough to make guesses about income and purchasing habits. This kind of analysis is called demographics, and uses a scale familiar to anyone who reads the business section of a newspaper: A (professional), B (managerial), C1 (junior managerial), C2 (skilled manual) etc.

A refinement of this system is called geodemographics, which includes more transient information – what shops there are and what they sell, what the average house costs, what cars are parked outside, etc. Just this kind of analysis is a great advantage over ordinary television, and the internet.

"It's not like a PC," says Phil Swain of Cable and Wireless, "where you can log in on any machine and you're in there. Obviously, set top boxes don't move. They stay at number 32 Acacia Avenue. So we know that the subscriber is Mr and Mrs Jones with their daughter Emily, and this is the demographic profile they're in, because of either their CACI ranking or the information that they volunteered for us."

But instead of just buying in profiles of neighbourhoods, broadcasters will soon be able to sell them. Every night their computers will be able to name the towns that eat the most caviar and the streets that spend the most time following the stock market. No surveys required. And, for that matter, why should they aggregate individual purchases into broad geographic categories when they can do even closer analysis on the activities of a single household?

Lifestyle Data

If it is not necessary to guess what people buy, a marketer can start guessing what kind of shoppers they are.

Lifestyle data turns subscriptions, memberships and purchases into consumer profiles. Buying things online is an especially good way to answer such questions as "What newspaper do you read?"

and "What kind of alcohol do you offer when you are throwing a party?" When your choices fit a certain pattern of consumption, they indicate what else you will buy.

Such links can be practical, like the one between charcoal and barbecue sauce. Or they can be tied to an outside factor that drives people to buy, like a link between garage door openers and high powered lawn equipment. All over the world there are companies which exist solely to collect lifestyle data. Some send out their own surveys, others gather information from people who thought it was being used for something else. In America, a firm called Abacus Direct hold information from more than 2 billion catalogue purchases.

And in a sign of how things are going, this company is now merging with a firm called DoubleClick, which tracks the movement of people on the internet. The goal is to link the named, addressed catalogue data to the previously anonymous web surfing. DoubleClick's competitor, 24/7 links its web surveillance to the names and addresses of people who go online to register their new computer products.

It's all very tricky. But this subterfuge is only necessary because companies like DoubleClick and 24/7 do not already have the address of every single user, and do not own the entire network of cables, servers and the software running into every set top box, nor do they have final say over what users can and cannot do. The providers of interactive television will have no such limitations.

Within a system entirely under their control, they will note everything you purchase or show interest in purchasing, every group you join or just visit. A lifestyle profile can be assembled from such telegraphic behaviours as these:

- the amount of time you choose to spend watching TV
- the number of TVs in your home
- the amount of pay per view TV you purchase
- the types of programmes you watch
- the amount of email you send
- the answers to any surveys you answer, whether on paper or on the screen.

Roger Randall of Agency.com explains how your viewing profile could be used to provide leads to an airline:

"You would probably have target programmes in mind. If you were British Airways for example, and you had an executive recruitment scheme, I'm just thinking on the fly here, you might earmark Newsnight, news at 11, plus the gardening show. And if households were to watch all three of those programmes, you might as well send them a mailer. Because that, plus the postcode data, would start to feel like a profile."

And, just like the profiling companies on the internet, the interactive TV providers will have the opportunity to link to outside databases. Phil Swain of Cable and Wireless gives a similar hypothetical example. This time, a viewer has clicked on a discount offer:

"Well, not only have we given British Airways a list of all the names and email addresses of the people who have responded to that, but we also know a lot more about those people. We happen to know they watch these kind of programmes, they also bank with this kind of bank, they also purchase these kind of products and all that kind of stuff."

When Swain uses the phrases "kind of programmes" or "kind of bank", he indicates the importance of using categories to hold all the bits of viewer behaviour. Someone had to sit down and decide what these categories were – the kinds of programmes shown by Cable and Wireless, the kinds of banks their viewers could do business with, the kinds of commercials to be shown.

For a number of reasons, broadcasters have always used these classifications. They might want to avoid airing commercials for two soft drinks in the same programme. Or they might want tell an advertiser how many viewers of "daytime dramas aimed at housewives" also watch "daytime dramas aimed at schoolchildren". With digital interactive television gathering so much information, classification becomes more important than ever, and it can be done in greater detail.

More importantly, it can now be done by a machine. A few years ago, a computer at a large supermarket noticed that diapers and beer were being bought together in large numbers, after 5pm. As it happened, men who drove out to get diapers in the evening were picking up beer at the same time. When this supermarket promoted beer and diapers near each other, sales went up.

This link between beer and diapers was found by a technique

called data mining, which means attacking large amounts of data with artificial intelligence, or as it prefers to be known these days, neural network software. Instead of a salesman or a sociologist trying to guess what new types of consumer may exist, the neural network software just runs through the gigabits of sales data and looks for patterns. Then, sounding like a stand-up comedian, the computer asks: "Hey, did you ever notice that people who buy diapers after 5pm always buy beer? Why is that?"

Notice, it was not necessary to answer the question. Lifestyle analysis is just behaviour responding to behaviour: You like beer and diapers? Fine. Here's your beer and diapers right next to each other. If you start buying car anti-freeze, we'll put that in the same aisle as well.

Neural networks will be used with digital interactive television in a number of important ways. This first is called collaborative filtering. And if you ever buy books on the internet, you can see it at work. Search for the book *1984* by George Orwell at the online bookstore Amazon.com and the page you get informs you, down at the bottom, that

> People who bought *1984* also bought:
> *Animal Farm* by George Orwell
> *Brave New World* by Aldous Huxley
> *Fahrenheit 451* buy Ray Bradbury

To come up with this advice, the software has been observing all people who buy all books. As more Amazon customers are seen buying the same two books, you can imagine those titles moving closer together on some virtual map. Eventually, clusters of titles appear, and the computer has invented a category of book.

Click any of these titles and you can buy the books yourself, on impulse. Like the beer and diapers, the sales tactic is simply to put the products people buy next to each other. It can all be done automatically.

Howard Hughes, advertising manager for NTL's interactive division, describes how collaborative filters will work on television, where they will be promoted to viewers as "intelligent agents" helping you to discover the programmes and services you would like to have.

"You'll be watching TV and it will offer you things," he says. "You may think 'I don't want that', and you watch it, and it will be great. And you'll say 'How did they know I'd like that?'"

Sounds nifty. But you have to ask what else your intelligent agent has been programmed to do, and who else it is helping. To create these top-of-the-pops lists of the population's favourite books, Amazon collects data on individuals, which could then be put to many other uses. Even aggregated data, reported in groups without names, can put the individuals analysed at a disadvantage if it has a fine enough granularity – that is, if the groups of individuals are small enough to be recognised and targeted.

Amazon had some bad publicity recently for just this reason. After offering a service whereby customers could view lists of best-selling books broken down by companies, they were flooded with angry calls from firms who did not want their competition knowing what their executives were reading.

Amazon wasn't seeking to make any direct financial gain from their service. But the categories of product you like are something else that TV providers can sell to British Airways. Companies are very excited about this software. It is why so many of them are keen to build what are called "data warehouses", stuffed with every computer transaction in the whole business. But none of them will have television's daily, intimate relations with members of the public.

What you do with your TV will fit you into clusters of activity that extend far away from your television, to areas of your life you thought were yours alone. To an extent you never thought possible, what you like and don't like to do will become known, and even predictable.

Segmentation

Lifestyle analysis is a powerful way to look at your behaviour. But staring at these clusters on our virtual map does beg the question: Who are these people? If we're creating categories, then what kind of person is reading *1984* and *Fahrenheit 451*? Are they just people who like books with numbers in the titles? Many of your actions are linked not to each other, but to you, and some set of reasons you carry around for doing and buying things. Mapping these reasons requires a different kind of analysis.

Used loosely, the term "segmentation" just means breaking down any market into chunks. But the chunks that companies really want look typical of people we all know. Market segmentation seeks to go beyond a consumer's buying decisions and round out his or her profile with attitudes and perceptions. Fur coats and diamond rings, or hunting rifles and pick-up trucks are not just linked, they are badges of certain personal styles.

When applied to cars, alcohol and ice cream, this information is vital to advertisers. They want to know which people think their product says something meaningful about them. Or they want to define a product that appeals to certain types of consumers.

When applied to TV shows or online services, market segmentation is doubly meaningful. Consider that every programme is also, to some extent, a commitment to think certain thoughts and spend time with certain imaginary people, and it is easy to see that what you watch will say more about you than your choice of detergent.

It can hint at the answers to such questions as:

- What anxieties do you have in your life?
- What is your attitude toward sex?
- What issues will determine how you vote in the next election?
- How would you define a healthy family?

These are not questions about soft drinks, and yet the makers of soft drinks might want to know your answers. They describe the way you choose to live.

One thing market segmentation, or niche marketing, seeks to know are the groups you belong to — clubs, societies and sports etc. But television itself is now shown to be responsible for a huge decline in such local participation. And it is interesting to note that as fewer and fewer people join others for any common purpose, there are more and more groups that people belong to without knowing it.

Tesco, the first supermarket chain in Britain to introduce a loyalty card scheme, used it to define 21 types of Tesco shopper. If you are carrying one of their cards, they will be using it to place you into one of those groups. This year, the BBC began something called its "100 Tribes" project, hoping to create a similar classification of all its viewers.

The purpose of such groups is, of course, sales or public relations. And more than just products, the practitioners of this analysis can then sell whole ways of life that just happen to include all sorts of objects to buy and opinions to hold.

Notice the progress here – from your neighbourhood to your grocery cart, to your home where you live and think a certain way. And as the information gets more intimate, it gets more difficult to collect. Nobody could play this game with just names and addresses. Until recently, the analysis of niche markets was used only for creating brand identities in the public eye, or selling directly to people who had chosen to associate with like minded people.

So, for instance, you could create a "sexy ice cream" and hope that a certain type of person noticed it on the market. Or you could directly sell a range of goods to members of an organised group like the Mormon church. But you couldn't find and target the people who would just happen to want sexy ice cream.

Another example: you could write a commercial encouraging people holding certain political beliefs to sterilise themselves, and hope they responded. Or, you could directly target members of a particular political party with "10% Off Sterilisation!" coupons, mailed to their homes. But you couldn't find and target all the people who just happen to hold certain political beliefs. Interactive television has been created, from the start, to overcome such limitations. Every single viewer can be linked to a segment and every segment's individuals can then be reached in any number of ways.

"The potential is absolutely enormous," says Howard Hughes of NTL. "You're dividing up a mass market and reaching them as individuals – it doesn't get any better than that."

Think of all the different "tribes" who could be targeted:

- Households with children
- Households with children who get anything they want for Christmas
- Households with children who seem to move between two houses
- Households where one member of the family is likely to be an alcoholic

- Individuals who take part in political demonstrations
- Individuals likely to be critical of government policy
- Individuals who fear people of other races

But the tribes or segments to which Winston Smith belongs need never have existed in a marketer's imagination. Here is the second important application of neural network software to digital interactive television: it can be used to help segments of the population find themselves. This is a version of the clustering technique described above. Except instead of clustering actions around people, the Watcher clusters people around the things they do, or products they buy, or opinions they hold.

The Amazon.com website features the use of this application as well. If you go to a service of theirs called "Book Matcher", you will be invited to rate five books from a long list. The service is then able to recommend other books you might like. To come up with these recommendations, the computer uses the collaborative filtering described before. But in this case, when looking for clusters of products you might like, the computer pays more attention to purchases made by people who have already shown themselves to be similar to you.

So, for instance, if next to George Orwell's *1984* you selected "Loved it!", then the computer would pay more attention to the recommendations of someone else who liked that book, or someone who liked Ray Bradbury's *Fahrenheit 451*.

A company called Andromedia that makes this kind of software refers to these people as your "like minded peers", and Amazon.com also describe their Book Matcher "a meeting of minds". The funny thing of course is that you will never meet these other people you seem so well matched with, except on Amazon's terms. You have not come together for any purpose of your own, but instead have been identified as a segment of the population for someone else's purposes.

Who are you? What shall we call you and these like minded peers of yours? Well, along with every book, it is possible to cluster words, perhaps taken from book reviews, or some more systematic classification system. In your case, the phrases "political", "dystopia", and "chilling vision of the future" might be gathered together into a vocabulary which can then be used by anyone who talks to you, or about you. The computer has created its own market segment, and knows everyone who belongs to it.

Before computerised checkouts and loyalty cards, these patterns in retail behaviour were not very interesting. Now they are extremely profitable. The patterns created by people watching interactive television will be many dimensions more sophisticated. Your TV will record not just what you buy, but what you are thinking of buying, what you look at, what you turn away from, where you go and how long you stay there.

Do you think no one could be bothered to study all that? You are wrong. It is already being done. With data this good, and software this powerful, some marketers and PR men look forward to an era when they can throw away their marketing books and let the machines do the work.

Howard Hughes has spent his career talking to customers and non-customers, hoping to create messages that would appeal to them. "But now," he says, "We're moving away from that. With this technology, the statistics match themselves to the consumer. You don't need psychology exactly. I'd almost call it the de-personalisation of advertising. With the data that comes back, we'll remember everything about everyone. We don't need marketing know-how anymore, we need technological know-how."

Hughes could be called an empiricist. He believes that, in the future, people's actions will suggest their own marketing responses. But not everyone agrees with him. There are still theorists, who are just as excited about interactive television. They believe some of the psychology that Howard Hughes would leave behind is finally getting its chance to show off what it can do. These are the "deep guys", and suddenly everybody wants to talk to them.

Psychographics

Ever since psychology was first studied, people have sought to use it as a means of persuasion. And though no one could seriously say that marketing, advertising or public relations were sciences, neither could they deny the tremendous power that a knowledge of psychology has afforded them. One thing is for certain: no one is just dabbling. Anyone who claims that success in these professions requires only "good ideas" and "creative talent" deliberately ignores the research that is done into what levers control the human psyche. The study of "behavioural marketing" has been well financed, continually improved and is now a required element of any certified qualification in these fields.

So, before looking at how the theories have worked in practice, and how they will soon be made part of every television set, consider the following synopsis of "Behavioural Aspects of Marketing" written by Keith C. Williams for the Chartered Institute of Marketing, Europe's largest professional marketing body. His excellent guide helps students prepare for exams set by the Institute and for the Certificate in Advertising and Marketing (CAM). We apologise if these passages are a bit dry. Our aim is only to convey how seriously this subject is taken by people who create much of what you see and hear in the modern world.

How to Pass Your Chartered Institute of Marketing Exam Without Really Trying

Williams' book opens with a chapter about behavioural sciences in general and the **scientific method** of enquiry (**control groups, test groups,** etc.)

Then it moves on to theories of perception, with pictures of faces that become vases and ink blobs, illustrating **figure and ground**, the various theories of **perception** and **memory**. Key words you'll want to know are **cognition, gestalt, receptors, liminal, subliminal, absolute threshold, intensity, position, contrast, novelty, repetition, movement, expectation of awareness, divided into awareness set, evoked set, inert set and inept set, proximity, symmetry** and **closure**.

The next chapter defines the features of **learning**:

- creates change in behaviour
- the change is permanent
- the change is a result of experience

Main factors in learning are **association, reinforcement** or **reward,** and **motivation. Classical conditioning,** as first shown by **Ivan Pavlov** in experiments on a dog, involves following a **conditioned stimulus** (bell) with an **unconditioned stimulus** (food) to provide an **unconditioned response** which over time becomes a **conditioned response** (salivation). According to Williams:

"Classical conditioning is not just a laboratory novelty, but can be seen operating in everyday life. The housewife who purchases a new product, because of a price discount scheme, may continue to purchase the product even when the sales promotion scheme has ended."

A more sophisticated "**operant conditioning**" was first described by **B. F. Skinner**, using his "Skinner Box" containing animals, levers, food, water and electrical shocks. Basically, the more a rat (cat, dog, child) hit the right levers (crawled into the right places) the more **positive reinforcement** (food, sugar water) or less **negative reinforcement** (loud noises, electrical shocks) it receives.

Conditioning theories of learning are known as 'black box' theories, because they only model **stimulus** and **response**. They make no attempt to model the mental processes in between.

Williams describes the work of **Kohler** on **insight** (chimpanzees suddenly grasping a situation) and **Tolman** on **latent learning** (mice internalising a map of their maze) and then talks about **memory**, whose basic features are **encoding, storage** and **retrieval**. Especially interesting is a paragraph on "**depth encoding**". This refers to the amount and detail of sensory stimulus provided with a memory. The more you see and hear, feel and experience movement of something, the easier it is to hold it in your mind.

The **motivation** chapter of Williams' book is the most important. Here is where the black boxes open right up. Motives can be **physiological** (hunger), **primary** (The desire to explore, manipulate things, contact with others, talk... feel alive) or **learned** (prestige, power, approval).

Alongside these crude classifications are more sophisticated ones. The most important, **Maslow's theory of self-actualisation** was mentioned over and over by people working with interactive television.

Maslow's theory describes a **hierarchy of needs**. Imagine a pyramid. At the base of this pyramid are **physiological** needs, above them are **safety needs**, then **belonging needs**, **esteem need**s and, at the top, something called **self-actualisation**.

As effective as it is to put a poster on a subway platform in July saying "Hot? Thirsty? Drink Wave!", the new goal is to be able to say "Drink Wave, it's the drink for who you really are!" and have people believe it.

An interesting section is the one titled "**frustration**" and describes such responses as **sublimation, compensation, apathy, fantasy, regression, aggression (constructive, destructive, direct or displaced), fixation, repression, anxiety, reaction formation, projection** and **rationalisation**.

"How then can a knowledge of frustration help the marketer?" asks Williams.

To answer, it's best to do some **motivational research**, as pioneered by **Dichter**, the first person to use techniques of clinical psychology for marketing. Dichter is the man who started using **focus groups** and **depth interviews**. Since then, marketers have also used **thematic appreciation tests, Rorschach** blob tests and **free word association**.

"For the marketer", writes Williams, "an understanding of the process of motivation is of fundamental importance."

He goes on to say that motivation in the modern age is difficult even for individuals themselves to understand. If what's motivating you is no longer as simple as hunger, or fear of tigers, you might lose sight of why you do what you do.

"As motives become more complex," writes Williams, "The individual is less able to appreciate the motivational basis of his behaviour. Indeed, it appears that many consumers see the acquisition of a particular product, for example a car or a mink coat, as a goal in itself, and do not realise that it is only a means of satisfying a complex need."

See how the language of behavioural studies can be used for very different purposes. Like anyone learning to be a psychiatrist, or a Buddhist monk, the student of marketing is expected to know what difficulties people face when trying to make sense of their own lives. However, unlike a therapist or spiritual guide, the marketer's job is to make those difficulties even more seductive and confusing. Williams offers this counsel:

"By understanding the basis of higher order motives the marketer is better placed to influence the consumer's **goal-directed behaviour** to the purchase of his product."

So next time you are feeling that you don't know what will give you real happiness in your life, take a moment to thank the young men and women studying for their big test at the **Chartered Institute of Marketing**, whose job it will be to keep you that way for as long as possible.

Having considered solitary individuals, Williams moves on to describe the **social influences** on their behaviour. A **role** is an organised system of behavioural expectations. The organising is done by **institutions** and **associations** with groups. People will consume to fit their role, or a role they aspire to. **Ely Chine** described status as "a kind of social identification tag which places people in relation to others." Such roles are often tied to **class**, which brings us to **Jicnar's social grade definitions**:

A   upper middle
B   middle
C1   lower middle
C2   skilled
D   working
E   subsistence

A brief description of **culture** and **ethnicity** brings us to **groups**. These are important, as they influence not just the people who belong to them, but the people outside who hope to join or avoid them.

A famous experiment on groups was **Sherif's "autokinetic effect"**. He put a bunch of people in a dark room and asked them to describe the movements of a small light. It wasn't really moving. But after a while, anyone in that situation will start to see it move. The participants all talked about which way they thought they saw the light going. Interviews afterwards showed who in the group agreed with whom, who was the group's **opinion leader**, who were followers, and how these roles coincided with the participant's relative popularity in the group. Popular people had great sway over where the others saw the light "move".

Engel, Blackwell and **Kollat** identified the following **family life cycle stages**: bachelor, newly married, full nest I, full nest II, full next III, empty nest I, empty nest II, solitary survivor I, and solitary survivor II. Each stage has different amounts of money and buys different things.

F. Elkin described socialisation as "The process by which someone learns the ways of a given society well enough so that he can function within it." **Socialisation** prepares the individuals for the roles they will play and ensures continuity of the culture.

People are socialised by:

- the family
- school
- peer groups
- the mass media

The process of socialisation can work in five ways:

- conditioning and shaping behaviour, primarily with reward and punishment
- imitation of others
- identification with role models
- playing an actual role
- cognitive mediation – actually thinking about things

After an individual is socialised, **Allpaort** defines his **attitudes** as "mental and neural states of readiness". **Katz** identified four **motivational bases for attitudes:**

- instrumental or adjustive
- ego-defensive
- value expressive
- knowledge

They can all be measured with the following methods of measuring attitude: **Thurston's scale, the Likert scale, Osgood's semantic scale, Guttman's scalogram analysis, Kelly's repertory grid technique.**

Well known to marketers is **Fishbein's extended model:**

$$A\text{-act} = \sum_{i=1}^{n} b_i e_i$$

Where A–act is the attitude towards doing something. B_i is the individual's belief that doing that will lead to consequence i. An n is the number of important consequences. So, for instance, if someone says "I'm thinking of having myself sterilised," that person is imagining a story of visiting the clinic and having the snip. With

Fishbein's model, the marketer can examine at that story in his or her head and turn it into measurable quantities.

Osgood and Tannenbaum's congruity theory can be seen at work in the following scenario: someone you like praises someone you hate. How does it affect your thinking?

Festinger's theory of cognative dissonance describes the following predicament: you are not a coffee drinker, but you are enjoying a cup of coffee. What do you do now?

The following **qualities of a message** determine its effectiveness:

* Amount of discrepancy between original attitude and message
* One sided vs. two sided messages (Use two sided arguments for smart people and simple, one sided messages for everyone else)
* Repetition of message – This is what moves information from short to long term memory
* Fear Arousal – Janis and Feshbach found in 1953 that weak fear inducing messages are good for changing behaviour, but strong appeals to fear trigger psychological defenses, so the receiver blocks out the message.

(So, for example, this is too much: "Interactive television will spy on you in your living room! You'll have no privacy!" This is better: "Why pay to be spied on in your own living room? Privacy is cool!")

To change someone's attitudes, the marketer needs to know about **Hovland** and **Weiss's** work on the **popularity of the source** (people agree with people they like) and **Walster's** work on the apparent **disinterestedness of the source**, who should appear disinterested, like "an expert".

But soon after a message is delivered, it no longer matters where it came from. **Kelmen** and **Hivlan's** work on the 'sleeper effect' showed that, after a while, people no longer connect a message with its source. Once you're past an initial barrier of attention and hostility, people believe anything.

Williams looks at "The Individual Within Society". The traditional **"one step" model**, where information goes out to consumers, is replaced by a **"two step model"** where information goes out to **"influencers"** or **"opinion leaders"**, who are then terribly important.

They belong to the same group or class as the rest of the audience, but they are more sociable and self-confident. They adhere closely to group norms, but are keen to try new things. They have greater interest and knowledge of their area of influence and they have greater exposure to the media.

Marketers take great pains to find these people. "Resulting hopefully," writes Williams, "in the advertiser gaining a number of extra and unpaid salesmen."

Following these opinion leaders is a cycle of **diffusion of innovation**. Here Williams points out the importance of social networks – the inter-connected friends, co-workers and acquaintances who make or break a new product.

Rogers and **Shoemaker** tried to break them down into the following five categories:

- Innovators
- Early adopters
- Early majority
- Late majority
- Laggards

The marketer will want to find people in those first two groups and win them over. They bring along the rest.

To know his target, the marketer needs to study personality theory.

Freud's work is the most famous. Know your **id, ego** and **superego**, as well as your **unconscious**, defence mechanisms – **repression, sublimation** and **projection**, as well as your stages of **socialisation**: oral, anal, phallic, and genital.

But, as Williams points out, even if you agree with Freud, you can't really use him to sell things unless you have access to face to face analysis and projective techniques.

Easier to use is **trait theory**, whereby all the different ways to describe someone are boiled down to an inter-related few. The most famous is **Cattell's**, with 16 factors in two dimensions:

A Reserved – Outgoing
B Less intelligent – More intelligent
C Affected by feelings – Emotionally stable
E Humble – Assertive

F Serious – Happy-go-lucky
G Expedient – Conscientious
H Restrained – Venturesome
I Tough-minded – Tender-minded
L Trusting – Suspicious
M Practical – Imaginative
N Forthright – Shrewd
O Self-assured – Apprehensive
Q1 Conservative – Experimenting
Q2 Group-dependent – Self-sufficient
Q3 Uncontrolled – Controlled
Q4 Relaxed – Tense

Using questionnaires, such as Cattell's own **16PF test** (Sixteen Personality Factor Questionnaire), it is possible to plot where any individual sits in this "psychographic space". Although these categories are more descriptive than explanatory, as Williams points out:

"If a submissive person is one who always backs down, is it useful to say that they back down because they are submissive?"

Self-concept theory is more useful. A person perceives himself, as well as an **"ideal self"**. When the two are too far apart, he or she is unhappy and dissatisfied. So, individuals select what they see, trying hard to find a world which reinforces their self image. Everything we do is touched by this attempt to be consistent with who we would like to be. That applies directly to purchase behaviour.

Birdcall interviewed car owners and found them describing their vehicles with the same words they used to describe themselves. **London** did the same for nineteen categories of product and found that people bought every one of them in order to reinforce their self-image or their ideal self-image. Turn this around, and you have something very powerful. If the marketer knows what words you use to describe who you think you are, or who you want to be, he can use those same words to sell you carpet shampoo.

There is much more to Williams' book. It provides a concise, well written introduction to a fascinating subject – one that encompasses every part of human existence. Marketing is a great profession that literally runs the world.

Behavioural Marketing Gets Its Chance

In practice, psychology and sociology have helped professionalise all contact between institutions and individuals. The tricks of various trades for moving merchandise and gaining public attention can now be discussed in the language of behavioural science. Best practice has spread wider and faster, carried by a new breed of consultant whose techniques can be adapted to any organisation.

The depersonalisation mentioned by Howard Hughes has, of course, been a defining feature of the twentieth century. Instead of relying on individual human beings, people increasingly get what they need from companies, governments and even machines. Behavioural science has been used to give such powerful, impersonal entities a human face.

It has also created helped create the "consumer society". It allowed marketing to make the crucial leap from satisfying people's needs to creating them. Only in this century could any tradesman seriously talk about "shaping public perception" or been able to define his product in terms of "consumer self-concept". Systematic persuasion is now everywhere and companies offer entire lifestyles instead of just the products that once accessorised them.

For a while, these changes caused a deal of concern.

Remember *The Hidden Persuaders*? In 1957, Vance Packard wrote this book exposing the ways that American industry was using psychology to manipulate consumers, particularly through the use of messages hidden in commercials and magazine advertisements. The book was widely discussed at the time, and encouraged a new scrutiny of the advertising industry.

Since then, it has been forgotten. The story is old, people are accustomed to media seduction, and we all consider ourselves terribly sophisticated, immune from the manipulative techniques that Packard described. As members of the consumer society, we are willing to think, if not entirely believe, that our free will has remained intact. But if the post-war rise in cases of anorexia and bulimia in teenage girls has not already prodded them to do so, perhaps people will think again about Packard's book when they see how digital interactive television is to be used.

The tools of persuasion he described were, in fact, blunted by a certain unfortunate limitation. Effective at the high level, when creating new products or planning campaigns, behavioural marketing was stopped from operating at the low level, on the individual consumer, for whom it was originally invented.

The limiting factor is anonymity – a lack of intimate knowledge about who you really are. Keith Williams mentions it in his chapter on motivation:

"The main problem is that of attempting to study not only apparent and conscious motives, but also the unconscious and hidden motives of a highly complex social animal who exists in a dynamic environment... Thus there is a constant requirement for the marketer not only to be aware of all the motives governing action at any one point in time and their interrelationships, but also to be able to predict the nature and extent of changes. A complete picture is unlikely to emerge until research techniques become more sophisticated."

In other words, visit him twice a week for three years and your therapist may be able to break your string of disastrous relationships, or take away your fear of spiders. But all the 30-second spots and half-hour infommercials in the world cannot use that same knowledge of human beings, except in a crude and limited way, because the agency producing them just doesn't know you, the individual viewer.

Unless he can spend some time with you, speaking and listening to you alone, the practitioner of behavioural marketing is left scrawling the letters S-E-X on bubbles of carbonation in glasses of beer in magazine advertisements. He can grab your attention by any part of your body left uncovered, but once he has it, he doesn't know what to do with it:

Are you hungry? Do you like sex? Great, look at this! Ahh, but you want friendship. Well that becomes more difficult. What kind of friends do you want? Should they look up to you, or would you rather tag along with them? Should they be in groups, or in single conversation? Are you in the mood for jokes, or do you feel like getting something off your chest? As copy writers move up your pyramid of needs, they find everything becomes very personal, and they can't quite touch you. Where opponents of psychotherapy can accuse it of being a kind of rape or prostitution, behavioural marketing has had to settle for comparisons with pornography.

Jonathan Plowden Roberts, of the Database Group consultancy in Bristol, sums it up: "You've got to be able to capture the information about that person. It's no good having a wonderful classification system or approach if you can't find a way of applying it."

Roberts' specialty is psychographics – a deliberate attempt to provide the more sophisticated research techniques that Williams said were necessary. It is a form of market segmentation based not on location, purchase behaviour, attitude or perception, but on the underlying mechanisms of personality. So instead of targeting a generic "mind of the consumer", marketers can now break a population down into the types of minds they are ready to target.

Psychographics is as big a fashion these days as one to one marketing. And the two are often linked. Right now, most brands provide the same service and public face to everyone. If they want to start speaking intimately to smaller and smaller groups of consumers, companies know they have to get better at listening, understanding and predicting what motivates those people.

One to one is a high risk game. It offers big payoffs to companies who get their psychographics right, and big losses if they get it wrong. We are now caught in an arms race, with all the big manufacturers and advertisers building up data and terrified that their competition has access to more. The invasion of your privacy is not just an unhappy result of sloppiness or curiosity. It is being driven by intense market competition.

Psychographic consulting is an exploding field. And to get in on the action, you just need three things:

- A big computer
- Lots of raw data about individuals and households
- A system

Almost inevitably, the system is Maslow's hierarchy of needs. What attracts marketers to Maslow is his theory's elegant simplicity and its easy application. Where Freud's analysis requires access to an individual's life history, Maslow's classifications of need are easier to see, peeking up from beneath the answers to a questionnaire. The industries that specialise in modifying and reinforcing behaviour are very excited about this. And what's great about the needs Maslow described is their control over us. We respond to them before we know what we're doing, before we can intellectualise reasons that sound good.

Jim Brakin is the creative director at Amhurst, who provide a psychographic tool called the Motivation and Attitude Profile (MAP). He told *Direct Marketing* magazine:

"People are driven by their emotions: it's not about fact and logic. Increasingly, the only button you press is an emotional one. You find out what the needs are and you discover ways of reflecting those needs."

Everyone has something that makes them receptive to persuasion. For some, it's fear of danger to themselves. For others, it's the fear of being alone, or the fear of failure. Maybe in your case it's rats. Whatever it is, the person to find it is Pat Dade. His company Synergy Consulting are leaders in this field because their philosophy and approach are so incredibly ambitious. Dade describes a whole chain of causation that determines what a person does, and which his company follows from the inside out:

"If we can understand the values, beliefs and motivations of someone, we can begin to understand the attitudes that they adopt. And out of those attitudes come a whole collection of behaviours that people call "lifestyles" and then from there we can begin to understand the kind of behaviours exhibited within that lifestyle. So we actually don't start with behaviour, we end up with behaviour."

Not content with just Maslow's categories, Synergy creates its own by sending hundreds of thousands of questionnaires every year into the large companies who are its clients. Every questionnaire tests for the seven types of need in 60 different ways for each, making each questionnaire 90 pages long. Not content with the attitudes of a generic "outer directed person" or generic "sustenance driven person", Dade's company has also done 25 years of primary research on the attitudes of the British public. They are now in the process of creating similar categories for consumers in other countries.

"We ask 500 questions about you," says Dade, "So I'll know 'What's your attitude towards dogs?' I want to know about your sex, I want to know about your drugs, I want to know about your religion, I want to know everything. What's your attitude towards authority, how do you feel about family? We go into very, very deep depths before we start asking "Do you drink Coke?""

Obviously, anyone who buys your profile from Synergy is in a position to offer a great service, giving you everything you want, and lots of things you didn't know you wanted. But they will also know as much as they can about what it takes to change your mind or influence your actions. They'll know how someone like you should respond to different messages, perhaps even designed to scare or manipulate you.

What does it take to sell a burglar alarm to someone driven by security needs? What if you understood that person's values and their attitudes towards strangers, community and personal consumption? Throw in their address and likely income for good measure. What does it take to sell a pair of running shoes to a child who is driven by the need to belong?

Pat Dade knows the answers to all these questions. But that kind of bullying and seduction, he says, is old style branding – shouting and bragging at people, hitting them in their lower needs, not listening. Pat would rather move on to what he sees as the new style of branding.

He compares traditional advertising to the man in the singles bar who runs over to women, describes his sexual prowess in lurid detail and demands that they sample it, there on the floor with him. Relationship marketing, as the name implies, will be more sensitive.

His quick history of the subject runs like this: Until the 1950s, branding was just a guarantee that, like a McDonalds hamburger, any product of the brand would be of exactly the same quality. Then, with peace and plentiful food, a second type of branding appeared, promising people social acceptance or threatening them with loss of esteem. Obviously, both approaches are still in use. But Synergy's studies show that a solid 25% of people in Britain and America are not responding to these messages. In fact, as many as 35% of people are buying products not because of the way they are being promoted.

The reason, says Dade, is prosperity. After decades without war or famine, people now expect to live long and have interesting lives. They aren't excited by promises of hygienic food or envious neighbours. They want something more "authentic". And Dade sees this group growing. We are all moving up Maslow's hierarchy of motivations. And that is why Dade is so ambitious: he wants to sell right from the top of the pyramid.

Maslow's highest motivation is the need for something called "self-actualisation". It is your need to become who you really are, who you should be. So, for instance, there are now an increasing number of advertising slogans such as "Be yourself" or "Be anybody" or "For who you are" or, as supermodel Kate Moss advises the rest of us from her latest perfume poster "Just be".

If all this sounds like pop-psychology that's because it is. Both self-help writers and marketing men grabbed Maslow's theories and spread them into the general public. In the process, one to one marketing and psychographics were both invented. Listening to Pat Dade talk about identity, the real meaning of branding, and where people can fit Coke or Pepsi into their set of deeply held values, the whole subject again takes on that spiritual dimension. Dade is a genuinely charming guy. And you can just imagine his soft, Western American accent in your head, reading from that best-selling guide to personal growth that he could so easily have written.

He has even identified a target readership. Apparently, 8% of the population wish they could drop out of the rat race altogether. They have what they need and won't be fooled into thinking they need more. He calls them the "Tao Generation".

"These are people who know that enlightenment is actually possible," Dade says of his Tao Generation. "This isn't an airy fairy bunch of crap. And they don't have it. These are not enlightened people. These are people like us. I'm not saying that 8 or 25 percent of the population walk on water. But they're aware that they could. And they don't know how, and it pisses them off."

Dade, of course, specialises in selling them things. Synergy's goal, to capture the top of Maslow's pyramid in each person, differs from any other kind of marketing. To sell into someone's need for self-actualisation, you can't just offer them products. You have to offer them help on their own personal voyage of self discovery. And to do that, you have to know a great deal about each consumer, which is difficult.

To place people into their psychographic categories, and follow them over time, Synergy uses two very different questionnaires. The 500 question survey they send out is the one used to create Synergy's detailed psychographic classifications. Think of the hundreds of thousands of people who answer it as a laboratory. Dade breaks them down into what he calls "value groups" and can then ask them anything, put them in focus discussions or interview them individually, at length. "We talk with thousands of people," he says "and give them feedback: 'This is what we found out about you. Does it ring true or not?'"

When the categories have been defined and refined this way, the next step is to isolate some link between the value groups and the general population. In other words, what behaviour can be observed easily in millions of people, whom you don't know, that will identify them as holding the same values and beliefs as the thousands of people whom you know very well?

Answering questions is one kind of behaviour, and the second questionnaire Synergy uses is only 15 questions long. They represent points at which people of different psychographic types would have to start disagreeing. "One of the first things that comes out is opera," says Dade, "It really splits people. You're either an opera person or you're not. If you're an opera person, that gets rid of about 80% of people straight away."

Dade gives an example of how a short questionnaire can be used to profile a large number of people.

"There's a company called Claritas that does these shopper surveys. They've got like 12 million people on their database. And what we do a tie-up into their data, based purely on behaviour. We know the behaviour of our value groups, but we don't know the value groups of the 12 million people. And so we reverse-engineer back, using something like 120 different variables."

Understandably, after developing these questions that are accurate for a particular society, at a particular time in history, Synergy has them protected by copyright, so we could not reproduce them here. But you might start seeing them everywhere.

"This is happening to you already," says Dade, "Big companies are doing this." Apparently Shell now ask you to answer Synergy's fifteen questions to get their Smartcard. The 15 questions have also been put to everyone flying on British Airways. "The thing that we're trying to do now," Dade continues, "is with major insurance companies, because they have a big problem: they've always had accounts but never had people. They've insured 'an account' somewhere. So anyone filling in those applications will soon get the 15 questions."

The next step, of course, is to link this sophisticated analysis with the sophisticated technology now moving into people's homes. Dade is looking to put his 15 questions into a browser plug-in, so internet users and interactive TV viewers can set up their own psychographic profile. He believes that today's misunderstood consumers will actually welcome the chance to be psychoanalysed by their televisions. He describes what they'll get after they fill in the online form:

"We're going to say 'Look, this is who you are.' But you can change. You can change the different settings if you want to. Or you can just leave it default... People want to see if you are actually talking to them. If an ad for Coke comes into my browser and it looks really naff, then it wasn't designed for me: 'No. It wasn't. Huh, Coke isn't who I thought they were.' You can actually see through the message. It helps you understand what's going on there."

Dade imagines savvy consumers judging a product by its company's ability to create branding or advertising that reflects their own values. He thinks one to one marketing will become the norm, something consumers use instead of it using them. Maybe he's right. If your psychographic profile were your property in this way, maybe it would encourage you to demand more respect from organisations, and the people they pay to influence you. It might make their efforts more transparent.

Then again, there is also something frightening about Pat Dade's vision. Little phrases buried in what he says make a person wonder what kind of relationship he wants. Consider the singles club analogy. Here is how Dade describes his own company's approach to that woman at the bar:

"You tell them what they want to hear. But you have to find out what it is they want to hear first. So you walk up and say: 'Hey, that's a great dress!' or 'Where did you get those shoes?' I'm not revealing anything about myself. I'm making you the centre of my attention, and I'm listening to who you are."

Nice line, but why not reveal anything about himself? Maybe one to one marketing is not the drunk who puts his hand up your dress. It brings you flowers and listens attentively to what you say on all your dates. But why is it so keen to rummage around in your old letters? Why the hurry to meet your parents, talk to your friends, take your kids to the zoo, share bank accounts, spend all your free time together and buy a house?

Is Pat Dade a stalker? Sure, he talks about empowerment, and what people want in life. But what does he want, and what power does he have? What motivates him? In interviews, Dade repeats the following statement over and over because, he says, it took him 25 years to understand how true it was:

"The basis of all marketing, the basic thing that we're all trying to do, and marketing is just part of humans' lives, relationships, whatever, is very simple: We're just trying to change or reinforce existing behaviour."

Isn't that romantic? How would you feel if your partner described your relationship this way? People complain about companies treating them like numbers. But are you ready for the alternative?

In the United States, a man lost his health insurance because he bought some heart medicine on his credit card and the transaction was matched against his insurance records. People worry how insurance companies might use biological or genetic tests on their policy holders. Should we be as concerned when companies want to test and categorise our personalities? In his essay on Telegraphics, Neal Muranyi suggests how consumers might be affected by the data taken from their TV sets:

"Such systems would allow, say, insurers to differentiate risk – averse conservatives from high-living show-offs, and then tailor both marketing messages and risk scoring systems accordingly."

Will psychographic profiles do for marketing what DNA tests are doing for medicine and insurance? If the only person who knows me is a machine, was it perhaps better to stay a number? The same question could be asked about Pat's browser attachment. What kind of person consciously judges a product not by its merits, or even its style, but by its commitment to telling anybody whatever they want to hear?

After describing how viewers would be given control by his psychographic plug-in, Dade starts predicting that they'll give up that control anyway, just as new internet users worry about the cookie files put on their machine, only until they just can't be bothered to reject them anymore.

"Now there is no central warehouse," says Dade, "because of the data protection act and everything. So it's going to be a little bit difficult. But, if we do it through their browser and they can protect it, OR NOT: "yes I do want to be sharing that with you". Well then that's fine. You can do that."

In other words, by adding an element of participation to this new, intimate type of profiling, Synergy hopes to get past data protection legislation, and at the same time get consumers used to the idea of sharing. They have a good chance of success. As Two Way TV learned from running many surveys, people trust their televisions. They love answering questions.

But even if you don't, even if you now make a solemn vow never to answer another question about your lifestyle, Pat Dade still might get the information he needs. Answering questions is only one type of behaviour that Pat Dade can study. He says he can get answers to his 15 questions without having to ask them, perhaps with the help of a smiling animated friend:

"We know that when we're playing games," he says, "we're actually being more of what we are on the inside. Well, we could offer 'Here's a little thing that will help you set up your interactive web browser.' ... Remember, it's the kids who are growing up that we're talking about, who see internet access as a friendly, dialoguey kind of thing."

Any video game of fantasy is ideal for observing people's values and motivations at work. Moving as animated characters through virtual environments, game players must overcome obstacles and interact with each other. The problems they face may threaten them physically, or trap them in moral dilemmas. If designed to do so, a game can deduce much from what character a player chooses to be, how they play, and how they learn to win.

Synergy has worked with Electronic Arts, a leading video game publisher. But their last project fell through when staff at Electronic Arts objected to what was asked of them and refused to work on it. Synergy are now hoping to work with browser makers like Microsoft and Netscape.

Even without a dedicated game or TV browser application to do his testing, Synergy will be able to link viewers to their control groups. The behaviour to watch is, of course, watching television. As Neal Muranyi points out in his essay:

"It is interesting how the psychographic system providers often describe their different social value groups in terms of the TV programmes they favour. The descriptive power of this data is therefore of quite staggering significance for the marketing professional."

And here is the third way that neural network software will be used to analyse viewers. It will find their telegraphic signatures.

The idea of a signature, or fingerprint, is very important in direct marketing. For example, a company selling gold jewellery will gather a sample of people and ask how likely they are to buy various products. When people show a predisposition to buy gold jewellery, the company asks more questions. Surveys and focus groups are used to pinpoint some easily observed behaviour that these people have in common. Do they all drive similar cars? Do they read the same newspapers? Once it is found, the sales force can be told to search the general public for people who exhibit this identifying behaviour. With luck, they'll also get access to car dealership mailing lists or newspaper subscriptions

"You just create that first picture of a person," explains Neal Muranyi, "And then you run that model against any number of sources to see how many more there are out there like that. Those techniques have been in ply for many years. We do it all the time."

What a person watches on TV will provide enough detail to act as a new kind of signature – that of his or her value group. Synergy records what people in its value groups watch on TV. Then collaborative filtering software maps out clusters of their viewing activity. Instead of searching for correlations that are meaningful in themselves (for example people who watch Pet Hospital and also watch Lassie reruns), Synergy isolates clusters of activity that might mean nothing at all, but are shared uniquely among members of a certain value group. These clusters act like the signature of the group, which can then be found in the general population.

Your viewing profile will link you, not just to groups such as "men" or "men over 35", but to groups such as "men over 35 who have a strong need for approval from their peers".

Pat Dade gives an example:

"Let's say the hypothesis is that an inner directed person, if they watched da–da–da would react in such and such a way. Now you can test that. You can test it at the end of each time, because you're starting with the question 'Can we change or reinforce behaviour based on this information?'"

There's that creepy line again. This man wants to put you into his machines as a person, not just a number. He wants to know all your values and attitudes, and then help you find yourself. But what's the goal all the time? What's he selling? Is Pat Dade a therapist or brainwasher? Is he a spiritual guru, or the leader of some new cult involving British Airways and Shell?

We leave that to the reader. What your Watchers intend will never be as important as the fact that they exist, and the capability they now have to get the results they want. Like Pat Dade, Neal Muanyi of the Database Group plans to study control groups who are linked to the general public by television. And like Synergy, they are now developing both psychographic and telegraphic methods. But Muranyi is happy to mix the working practice of theorists, like Dade, with those of empiricists, like Howard Hughes of NTL.

For instance, because online sales and responses to advertisements are themselves the behaviours he is hired to increase, Muranyi calls their numbers "hard data". Because the data is hard, he doesn't feel the need to use a theory. Like Howard Hughes, he allows the data mining software to throw up its own segments of consumer activity. But then, to further break down those segments, Muranyi plans do psychographic analysis on each consumer's telegraphic data. Because viewing patterns are not themselves desired behaviours, he regards them as "soft data", and places them into rigid theoretical categories, like the ones used by Pat Dade.

Interactive TV is new. But the work going on behind it is mature, and ready for action. "I think it could be very powerful," says Muranyi's colleague Jonathan Plowden Roberts, "For people who can crack the psychographic thing, not crack it in terms of develop a system, but get the information on their customers, that's when it's going to sing."

The information on you will be available the minute you put an interactive TV set in your living room.

"25 years ago you couldn't do it," says Pat Dade, "because the basic research hadn't been done. 15 years ago you could just about do it, but we didn't have interactive TV. We've only been able to do it in the last six months."

Now that he can do it, Dade gives an example of how things are going to sing:

"That's when the behaviour starts coming. Now that we know who this person is, we can tell from their interaction with the television that they use QVC or they use Discovery, more importantly during the breaks they're flipping around, they're not watching the ads at all, but they tend to look at the Fiat Uno ad every time it comes on. I wonder why that is? We can do that in real time."

Notice the way interactive television will change how organisations think about you. Instead of salesmen or "creatives" standing around wondering "What could we say that would impress a certain type of person?" behavioural consultants will sit at their computer screens asking "Why hasn't this guy at 32 Acacia Avenue bought yet? What stimulus would motivate him to behave differently?"

At a time when we have intimacy, and rely on intimacy, with fewer and fewer humans, should we always be grateful for computers that know us as people?

Psychographics is not the same as psychological research. Where a psychologist puts questions to a small sample of volunteers, hoping to extract a meaningful theory, someone like Pat Dade uses established theory to create questions for everyone, hoping to extract meaningful data about individuals themselves. Psychographics is not therapy. Where a therapist seeks to put an individual in control of his or her self, someone like Pat Dade seeks to obtain that control for his clients.

Synergy's aim is to discover your secret self, who you are deep down or wish you were. Then they'll make a place there for their clients, and, with any luck, you'll start behaving. It actually doesn't matter whether or not he can do it. What is alarming about anyone practicing psychographics and one to one marketing is that they plan to try. And when their end is so incredibly ambitious, and the competition is so fierce, what means will they not feel are justified? Even if they can't replace your personality, what else will they find to do with their profile of the one you have?

Time and Friends

At this early stage in the launch of interactive television, most companies are struggling just to provide a regular service to subscribers. Most providers admit they will not be able to observe or target viewers as they would like until the next software upgrade. But since software upgrades can happen any time, without even notifying the viewer, it is worth listening to their plans. It is also worth looking at two important trends in advertising and marketing that will shape what TV providers are likely to offer their corporate clients.

As mentioned before, one trend that everyone talks about is relationship marketing, otherwise known as one to one. This type of marketing requires large amounts of information about consumers, which interactive TV is able to produce. But, just as important, relationship marketers will need to update that information over the weeks and years. Their aim is to sell products and ideas to a customer over his or her entire life, so everything viewers see will be fit into long term strategies.

The other trend that everyone talks about is community. Marketers and advertisers are increasingly keen to find or create groups of people who identify with their products. They are learning to sell into groups of people – workmates, friends, schoolmates, family members. Interactive TV provides unique access to them.

Assuming these trends remain powerful influences in the marketplace well after the next release of interactive television software, the next two sections, Time and Friends, consider what information marketers are looking to gather.

Time

Interactive television providers have time on their side. They don't have to ask long lists of questions or develop games to get their information all at once, because once it is captured, any data they get will happily sit in their machines for years. Howard Hughes describes how his company is now able to take the long view of its customers:

"If a company can gather three or four bits of information about you every year, and hold on to that information over the years, then it's worthwhile. It creates a profile that allows them to target you accurately."

And at three bits of information a year, even Pat Dade could have his entire questionnaire completed by the time of a viewer's next new car, or the next election. And while many of the facts gathered about you will be relatively unchanging, like your address, lifestyle or personality type, your TV will also seek to follow the rapidly changing story of your life. Every life is punctuated with events that might cause a person to buy things, change brands or adopt new attitudes: the birth of a child, the first day of school, summer holidays, exam weeks, graduation day, first day of college, perhaps a car, travel, gifts for boyfriends, first day on the job, marriage, children etc…

"Are you planning to buy a house in the next twelve months?" asks Jonathan Plowden Roberts of the Database Group, "Yes? Well I can tell you now any DIY company, any electrical goods manufacturer would kill to get your name and address."

Anticipating these life events and exploiting them is called event-driven marketing which, until now, has been difficult to practice. There has been no reliable way to pick up the signals of consumer curiosity, fantasy and inquiry. No one could watch them budgeting, shopping and finally buying. Plowden Roberts thinks this is going to change:

"Once people start doing their grocery shopping through the TV, once people get familiar with doing this, then I think you'll find more and more manufacturers looking at it as a way of promoting their product on a time-sensitive basis."

Patterns will also emerge. For instance, every home goes through periods of spending, investment and austerity. The "feelgood factor" that lifts or sinks economies and political fortunes is actually the sum of hopes and disappointments in individual households. The people behind your television will be looking for indicators of your household's own political and economic climate.

Also, individual manufacturers will be looking to track each household's interaction with their brand. On any given street, some houses will just be hearing about the brand, others will be loyal users and others will be losing interest, perhaps thinking of switching. Interactive television will help identify which households are which.

For the complete picture, manufacturers will want to know how people inside and outside the house interact with each other.

Friends

Before mass marketing, the relationship of people to each other was crucial in any effort to sell or persuade. Not only did the salesman depend on word of mouth, but even the grandstanding politician depended on his message filtering out from a packed room to families around dinner tables and people in bars and street markets.

Mass media, especially television, was able to leap over these social networks and plug viewers directly into a political or brand message. Interactive television will offer marketers the best of both worlds – mass market messages pumped straight out to the isolated viewer in his or her living room, followed by techniques of observing and even manipulating the social networks where viewers talk to other viewers.

The first relationship to aim for is with individual viewers, that ideal market segment of one. For this reason, it is imperative that television providers be able to identify who is watching a television at any given moment. A number of them have noted how difficult it is to develop a system of passwords or ID codes that viewers will faithfully use. And without such identification, it will be much more difficult to create any kind of viewer profiles below household level.

"That's a big big battle," says Jonathan Plowden Roberts of the Database Group, "to get people to register when they walk in and out of the room."

Expect to see the following types of services offered under slogans such as "TV the way you like it!" They will customise the TV screen to individual viewers. But at the same time, they will be signaling to the television provider that the individual is sitting in the room at that moment:

- Your own desktop, colours, wallpaper, shape, or window configuration,
- Pager service to alert you when you have email, or a friend is watching
- On-screen icons, allowing you quick access to all your favourite services – weather, news, stock prices etc.
- Programmes you might like, selected for you by your EPG. And "just to stop arguments around the TV", the EPG will offer to make suggestions about what programmes will be most acceptable to all the household members in the room at that time. (As long as all those members have logged on...)
- On screen tools that can be added or removed for people's preferences – email, shopping, calendar etc...

Expect advertisements for these customising services to emphasise the advantage of logging in and out of the room, moment by moment:

"Don't miss a great show because your EPG didn't know you were in the room!"

"Don't miss a great cartoon because the EPG thought your mom or dad was watching with you!"

Providers will aim to create a new relationship with the television, where you only feel really comfortable in front of it when you know it knows you are there. As Howard Hughes of NTL says, "Why would you want to watch TV with your sister's preferences?" In fact, all interactive marketing depends on creating this demand for customised service.

Rishad Tobaccowala of Giant Step, an interactive marketing firm, put it this way:

"In direct marketing, you make a spear, hunt down the consumer you want, and impale him. In brand advertising, you make a really, really sharp spear, chuck it into a crowd of consumers and hope it impales as many as possible. With online marketing you make a spear and invite the consumer to come and impale himself."

Once you are impaled, the next relationships for your TV to create or exploit are the ones you have with other people. From the TV provider's point of view, there are four types of social network to which you could belong. Each has its advantages and disadvantages as an avenue of marketing. The person selling or persuading will want to use the existing nature of the group – its ethos and power structure – to gain information about members and create incentives for members of the group to buy.

The first, involuntary formal groups, like schools or places of work, are stable and offer their own infrastructure for conveying messages, such as newsletters, meetings and teachers. But they may not attract the loyalty of their members. With luck, the power structure can be used as a way to access members without having to gain their individual permission.

The second type, self-selected formal groups, like churches or voluntary organisations, command great loyalty from their members, but the power structure of the organisation will be nervous of doing anything to offend them, and so have less flexibility to assist the marketer.

The third type, involuntary informal groups, such as people of the same race, religion or lifestyle are not so much networks as marketing segments. A structure of communication and shared activity must first be found or created.

The fourth type, voluntary informal groups, or friends, are the hardest to access, but the most fertile environment for sales. There are no member lists kept, no newsletters and no regular meetings. But to sell into such groups is the priceless "word of mouth" that marketers crave.

Interactive TV provides marketers with new ways to sell into all these groups of people:

- Questionnaires can be used to find out what organisations a viewer belongs to.
- Any special offer of TV service made through a school or workplace will identify the social relationship between members of that environment.
- A television can even identify informal friendships. It can ask people for names of friends, record which people play the same video game together, or speak in the same chat rooms.
- Cable companies have already been given complete lists of students. Matching these lists to a database of subscribers tells them what is happening at the playground level.

Any company that distributes advertising material in schools or offices is already counting on peer pressure to carry the group into sales figures that the individuals themselves would never yield. Interactive TV allows a gathering and coordination of word of mouth and peer pressure that no other mass marketing effort has been able to use.

The one social group to which every viewer belongs is the household, usually a family. Any advertiser that uses "pester power" techniques, which encourage children to get their parents to buy something, is using a knowledge of this basic social group.

Adam Soames is the marketing director of the marketing consultancy Abram Hawkes. His firm sell a software application they call PsyKey, which generates psychographic profiles, not of individuals but of companies. It helps suppliers work out their strategies for cracking the organisation and getting their product into the building, and regular use. PsyKey was developed for business to business sales, but here Soames describes how selling into a family is not much different:

"The whole family has an input, whether it be information gathering, or playing the role of the gatekeeper (which is usually the wife), right up to making the final decision, where the purse strings are. So you can actually see the family buying unit there."

Soames wrote his thesis on this idea, and listed the roles that various members of the family might take up in the process: initiator, influencer, decider, buyer and user. Then he gave an example:

"If the product needed was a new family car, then the initiator might be one of the children. The influencers might be the whole family and even friends. The decider might be the mother and the father. The buyer will either be the mother or father and the users will be the whole family."

Many companies now seek to exploit an understanding of how family buying units work. Every year, a conference called Kid Power draws managers of well known brands with the motto: "Strategies to successfully tap the buying power of children – and make them your customers for life!" Over two days, attendees hear such presentations as these:

- Marketing to Young Kids by Targeting the Gatekeeper
- Parents, Nagging Kids and Purchase Decisions
- Are We There Yet? – Selling Mom That a Day at Sesame Place is a Vacation
- What Works with Kids and Why: Child Psych-Based Ideation and Age Segmentation Integration

Another approach to households is offered at Family Power, another conference, where this year's presentations include:

- It's a Family Affair: A Hands-On Approach for Strategic Internet Marketing to Families
- Designing Integrated Family Promotions that Deliver: a Look at Denny's Kids and Family Campaign
- Achieving the Goal: Scoring with Families at the Grassroots Level
- Best Practices in Branding, Direct Response and E-Commerce: Case Studies of Online Ad Campaigns

Marketers are keen to understand where households get their information, how the members divide their shopping or reach joint decisions about shared purchases. They want to know what family members tend to agree with each other and who has final control over the money.

Surveys of different groups of consumers can begin to answer these questions. Sociological and psychological theory can be helpful. But the marketers who visit the Kid Power '99™ and Family Power '99™ have always faced the same problem as behavioural marketers – a lack of reliable information about their targets.

It is not really sufficient to print on the side of a bottle, as Pepsi does, "Ask for more!" and hope a generic child will tug on the sleeve of a generic parent. No family is generic. Each works differently. That is why interactive TV will be such a powerful new member of every family. Starting from such simple questions as "Who's name is on the credit card receipt?" and "Is it paid from a joint bank account?", an interactive TV can go on to answer questions such as these:

- How many televisions are there? How are they used?
- What kind of research is done before a big purchase? Who does it?
- Who makes the most impulse purchases?
- Who uses the TV most for information or research?
- Who spends the most time watching programmes?
- Who clicks on the most advertisements?
- Who seems most involved with the television?
- Who sends and receives the most email?
- Who is most politically active, and how?
- Given different combinations of house members watching TV together, who seems to have the most say in what to watch?
- How many kids are there?
- What do they like to do?
- What do they want for Christmas?
- Do they have their own televisions?
- How strictly do their parents supervise their viewing?
- When do husband and wife watch together, separately?

People love to answer questions about themselves, especially kids, and companies have been obtaining information from children over the world wide web for years now. Children's privacy legislation hardly slows them down. And any data gathered through the screen can be matched to lifestyle data that is bought in.

A family's data can be analysed by data mining software just as easily as an individual's. And when a computer has psychographic profiles of mom, dad and the kids, plus complete records of all viewing and buying behaviour, it will find patterns that identify the psychographics of the family.

Who are the opinion shapers in the house, for different issues and purchases? What is the best way to sell into the "Authoritarian Dad" home? What is the signature of the "Dad's away, Mom is overstretched" home? What are their names and addresses? Over time, interactive TV will have the answers.

Control

IT IS OFTEN SAID that one to one marketing is no different from the relationship you might have with a local grocer, who knows what you buy and gets to know your family.

But the only reason you would start talking to your local grocer is if you had come to trust him. And what if you found out that every time you left his shop he wrote down everything you said? What if you heard he was selling details about your family to people you'd never met? What if those people had worked out a set of experiments to try – things your local grocer was encouraged to do or talk about, in order to change your opinions, or what you did with your family in the evenings? What if your local grocer had huge resources available to gather more information and then conduct more experiments every day? Would you still trust this man? What if he asked to move in with you, staying in your child's room perhaps? He'd be just like one of the family, huh?

This is where things get really weird.

An interactive television does not just collect information about its viewers, but responds to what it finds, with all the power and resources available to the people who make and pay for television now. Instead of broadcasting the same signals to everyone, digital technology allows TV providers to push data and software to individual set-top boxes. The same computers which hold your profile will decide what ads to show, what programmes to offer and even what happens in those programmes. Neural network software will notice changes and formulate an appropriate response. Based on what you did last year, or five minutes ago, your TV will show you something different from what people are watching next door, or even downstairs.

Clearly, the benefits will be huge. Your TV will customise and personalise itself to your desires. It will learn to anticipate them and help you choose hours of programming. As you sit in your living room, relaxing, letting go, a world of information and convenience is going to open. But something has been hidden. And something big may be closing down forever.

The drawbacks of interactive TV are also huge. Any machine designed to react to your desires can also act on them for its own reasons, manipulate them and take advantage of them. Any computer that builds a lifelong profile of your family can do more than just remind you when a show you like is about to start. Any company that owns such a computer becomes a powerful influence in your life.

An interactive TV set will experiment on the people watching. It does this primarily by choosing the programmes, advertisements and services which are offered to individual viewers or groups of viewers.

This selection of programmes can significantly affect how you see through your "window on the world". A stack of crime shows and worrying news can make the world seem dangerous. A stack of escapism and colourful musicals can make the world look happy. A selection of TV can make your country look well or badly run, can make businessmen or the homeless or women or black people look good, evil, stupid or mysterious.

Of course, such selections are made now, and debated in government, academia and the media itself. Minorities in the US have recently complained at the way they are portrayed on TV. The Media Lab at the University of Glasgow has been documenting the extent to which the mentally ill are misrepresented. News values are always being questioned.

But with interactive TV, no two people need ever be shown the same thing. So who will be able to debate what you are shown? Computer algorithms will determine what appears on your screen, and you'll have no way to find out how they work. They will change all the time, depending on what arrangements have been worked out between service providers and their partners.

Targeting Strategies

As shown in the previous chapter, what makes interactive TV a powerful way to observe you is not the buttons you click, but the methods of analysis that can be aimed at those clicks. Similarly, the list of features that interactive TV is able to change for each set top box is only as powerful as the logic that makes those changes.

The subroutines and functions which spin to life behind each viewer-generated event are not just collecting data. They are responding to it. And their actions are co-ordinated on a grand scale – through channels, across platforms, between friends, and over entire lifetimes – always in conjunction with a long term business plan.

Having looked at the most important ways to analyse viewer behaviour, we now look at the main techniques that will be used to control it.

Simple Fit

For decades, databases have been filling with information about you. But it has been impossible for a television to reach you without reaching everyone else at the same time. The first technique then is just to use individual addressing to send different content to different television sets. In its most simple form, you will see news and information that is selected for your area, your neighbourhood, school or street. You may also be asked to volunteer information about what kind of programmes and

How an Interactive TV Can Respond

Like a web page, interactive TV will offer different services and entertainment all over the screen, all the time. What you watch, what buttons appear, and what happens when you click one, can change in the following ways:

Programmes offered: Everyone will see their own trailers, teasers and pop-up reminders. When they tune in to a show, they may even see their own version of it. This techniques will be especially effective where product placement is used.

News: Any programme or service that offers information can be customised into special issues, local editions and individualised bulletins. Headlines, pictures, text and video can all be changed from minute to minute, person to person.

Commercials: Anything that sells something will be targeted to people who might buy. Infomercials can be tailored to provide different information to each viewer, depending on what is likely to influence their buying decisions.

Branding: Product logos and product related images will be placed on your screen when and wherever they are most effective. Advertisers are especially keen to exploit online services and children's games. Look for the use of "virtual billboards".

services you like. Then, more of that content will be offered.

Individual addressing gives you more of what you want. But it also allows your Watchers to use their warehouses of data, starting with your name. You know all that junk mail you get now? All those letters that begin "Congratulations Winston Smith of Flat 7D Victory Mansions! You have already won a timeshare holiday home!" Do you wonder how they got your details? Well prepare to get much more of those letters, and emails, and phone calls. And watching interactive TV itself will be like reading junk mail for four hours every day.

Anything that can be personalised will be. Fake friendship is the world's oldest profession and cartoon characters in cereal advertisements will be able to call your children by their names.

Tools: A wide variety of online services will be offered by interactive TV. Expect them to be products in their own right, with special versions for boys, girls, working women, teenagers, retired men, etc.

Games: Aside from children's video games, many services and entertainments will feature 3-D environments where viewers can pretend to walk, run, jump or lie around. What games are offered and what viewers encounter in these virtual spaces can all be customised and changed on the fly.

Forums and Chat: Email list services, message boards and virtual chat rooms can all be offered to different viewers. The subjects for discussion, the participants and what they are allowed to submit can all be controlled. In some chat rooms, viewers will be offered a choice of on-screen personality to inhabit.

Online Transactions: Shopping and banking through your television will be entirely customised to (or targeted at) you. What you are offered, how much it costs and how much you pay will all change from person to person. You will be offered exclusive discounts and special offers.

Offline: Service providers and their marketing partners are not limited to responding on your television screen. In response to what you do with your television, you may receive email, pop-up messages, mail by post or telephone calls. How people in the real world, outside, respond to your viewing is limited only by their imaginations and the law. Most times you won't know it is happening.

You will be introduced to all sorts of "personal guides" and "viewing buddies" – anything to help simulate a friendship between you and your TV will be used. "Anthropomorphism," says Pat Dade, "is going to make a comeback." Yes, it will make some things easier for you. But yes, it will also be designed to play on your emotions.

The next bit of information to use is demographic and lifestyle marketing data. If you live in a wealthy neighbourhood, your TV will start offering you big cars. If you live in an Asian neighbourhood, you will see more advertisements for rice and fewer for mashed potato mix. You may see commercials for soap powder that feature Asian families. If you tell your television provider that you are Irish and your wife is Pakistani, you may see advertising aimed at two ethnic groups.

Then again, whether you tell anyone or not, your television may be able to find out. Your telegraphics might give you away, or your television provider might just pay someone for the information. Jonathan Plowden Roberts of the Database Group stresses again how important it is to have the right information:

"You as a brand might buy the slot at 7:17pm on a Tuesday evening, right in the middle of Coronation Street. The people who watch that are going to get 23 different messages. But you have to know who each person is. That's always the problem."

Using just a name and address, anyone with a database of subscribers, consumers or club members can match their list to your digital television subscription. Your TV provider can take full advantage of any available data from any source, perhaps trading data with one of the many companies that exist solely to collect lifestyle information.

So if you have children in school and buy them clothes through catalogues or subscribe to a parenting magazine, you may start seeing commercials for amusement parks. Your television provider will have matched data with the catalogue company, the magazine publisher, and even the school. The cable company Telewest, for instance, got access to children's home addresses as part of its Cable in the Classroom scheme. Any trace you leave in the outside world may soon affect what you see on television, and vice versa.

"Companies already spend a great deal of money on advertising," says Howard Hughes, "They have all this data about customers, but they've never been able to break host markets down and aim advertising and products to groups of people."

It won't just be advertising. Any service, and anything that can be customised, can be offered to advertisers as a way to reach viewers. An internet service called GoTo puts whatever website pays the most at the top of its searches. When your electronic programme guide (EPG) says "Here are some shows I thought you would like!" perhaps they will have been chosen this way.

Of course, it has always been possible to target a certain audience by advertising, say, toys during cartoons or aftershave during football games. Broadcasters have always coded their programmes to help advertisers place their messages efficiently. But programmes broadcast to unknown viewers could only ever be classified by guesswork. In the real world, where women watch football and adults watch cartoons, direct marketing on TV was impossible.

Now it is households and individual television sets that will be coded. The TV set in Winston Junior's room might show ads for a certain toy, no matter what programme he watches. Any television in the house can start showing ads for aftershave as soon as Dad logs in. Television providers will be able to sell your attention to advertisers with an accuracy never before possible.

Let's say the maker of a floor wax wants Winston Smith to see one of its advertisements. In the past, a TV set didn't know when it was on, what programme was being watched, or who was watching. Now it does. Soon his TV set will even know what parts of a programme he has seen if he stops watching it half way through.

So a television provider is now in the position to promise the floor wax company that Winston will see one of their commercials. If he doesn't see it tonight, the commercial might run first thing when he turns it on tomorrow. If he changes channel, the commercial could follow him, or another version might be shown later.

Now put together all these coding and individual addressing techniques. If you can show coded commercials during coded programmes to segmented audiences watching coded TV sets, you can fire specialised material at targeted individuals just when they are experiencing exactly the emotions you choose for them. Howard Hughes of NTL sets the scene:

"There's always been coding," he says "Broadcasters have always had to have codes to define advertising and programmes. What's changed is the level of sophistication. You're coding what's actually happening on the screen and when."

Behavioural marketing companies will be tapping their stores of psychographic information to match advertisements to viewers. Do you well up with emotion during medical dramas? Does news about social issues get you riled? If a child is hit by a car during a soap opera, are you more likely to blame the driver, the parents, the government or just fate? Advertisers will want to know as they choose messages to show people like you, at exactly these moments during the programmes you watch.

"You're actually choosing the mindframe you want for that person," says Howard Hughes, "and then offering the advertisement at that moment."

Simple Response

For someone in an office to aim an advertisement or programme directly at you is just the beginning. The next step is for the advertisements to aim themselves. Since it decides what to offer based on data it collects itself, any interactive TV is not just targeting, but responding to its viewers. So, as well as writing different content for different households, television providers will be writing computer programs that decide on the fly what to show on the screen, and this opens the door for more sophisticated techniques of persuasion.

"The interactivity," says Howard Hughes, "will act as an automated agent, using marketing experience to sell products to you individually."

The simplest form of a TV responding to you is the re-use of content which works. Television providers will compile a list of everyone who watched, or clicked on, or bought something from a particular advertisement. And next time those people watch TV, they might be shown the same ad, or a similar ad, or a different ad for the same product.

Anything can be clustered, and all the various behaviours in your telegraphic profile will be used to cross-fertilise each other. What you buy will influence what you watch, and those two things will influence what commercials you see and so on. Virginia McMullan of NTL gives a simple example:

"Let's say you watch every nature programme," she says "and it becomes clear you're a nature freak. Well, we can say "Here, buy this organic food or environmentally friendly washing powder."

The advertisers may specify which ads are shown to whom in what order, or the computer may wander among the items clustered around each household's purchase and viewing history. Since commercials themselves are just more items for viewers to select or reject, they will also end up in clusters. Collaborative filtering can then be used to show each television the commercials that have evoked a response from people who act or think like the people watching it.

The programmes themselves will be promoted this way, just as books are now promoted on Amazon.com. And Phil Swain of Cable and Wireless re-emphasises how "viewer choice", which everyone talks about, is actually a problem, now overcome with technology:

"As the data tracking facilities – capturing and profiling and mining and so on – give us the ability to build up more sophisticated profiles of the consumer, you can start doing push programming rather than pull. Where at the moment consumers are actually choosing, you'll obviously be presenting stuff that is already profiled for them, whether that's advertising messages or programming or what have you."

The next important step is to branch out, into your market segment. Once you have expressed interest in one product, advertisers can offer you other, similar products. Or, depending on what they know, they can offer you other categories of products that fit your tribe.

"If you find a profile of people who buy Beatles albums and Jimi Hendrix albums," says Howard Hughes at NTL, "and then you see some of them buy a purple cup, you then turn around and show all the people who bought Beatles and Hendrix albums that cup and I can guarantee sales will increase. No psychology needed."

If you have been offered something that other people within your profile buy, but you have refused it, then your television, like any salesman, will take a new approach.

"Probably the hottest thing in discussion at the moment is dynamic prices," says Robin Melvyn of NTL, "Let's say I look at a customer and realise they are not using an interactive service as much as they should do. They look like they belong to that segment, but for one reason or another, they're not jumping in."

Melvyn says he might then have the TV offer them three months free service to get them on board. Virginia McMullan gives another example of how your TV set will be ready to negotiate:

"Maybe it will calculate that this viewer likes this type of service or always buys this. Maybe we can upsell here, move him on to a premium range product and spend a little more."

Anything on your TV set that offers to sell you something might include simple logic to move on price, selection or terms of payment. Like a car salesman, your TV will be aiming to bring you around and talk you up to the deluxe model.

"There's a number of things you can do by way of offering them inducements," says Melvyn "to get them to behave in the way you want them to behave."

That is what this machine has been designed to do. And its work is made easier by the information it gathers about you as you sit on the couch, letting your mind relax. Home shopping programmes, which now offer the same products at the same prices to everyone, will know who watches longest, who spends the most, and who is most itchy to buy that last limited edition "Border Collie in Flowers" figurine.

What products make you salivate and just how few will be left before you are overcome by your itch to hit the "Add It to My Shopping Cart" button depends on what kind of person you are. This brings us back to psychology, and after reading the answers you give to their questions, and analysing exactly how you watch and what you buy, the behavioural marketing men will be ready to respond.

Watch as the techniques described in Williams' book are applied in anger to a quarter of your waking life. If you exhibit the behaviour of an "early adopter", you will be offered "new", "cutting-edge" porcelain figurines. If your desire for security is the strongest motivating force in your Maslovian hierarchy of needs, police officers will be selling you deodourant. Interactive content will enable "deep encoding" of soft drink images while the variables in Fishbein's extended model are finally given values, just for you.

Try it yourself! Turn back to the section of this book that described behavioural marketing theories. For each one, ask yourself: "How could I put this into a commercial, a programme, a game or a service, and then measure viewer response? What would I show next?

Everything your television does will be customised to your personality, meeting and suggesting needs at the highest possible level of self-actualisation. All the words you use to describe yourself, and who you want to be, will also, somehow, apply to various detergents and automotive care products. Your window on the world will show you anything you want to see as its sponsors move deeper into your life.

This is why direct marketing companies are suddenly powerful players in the television industry. The expertise they have, that everyone now wants, is their decades of collecting data, provoking responses and then going back to selected consumers with better targeted messages. These companies don't just "spread the word", they conduct experiments on people.

Evolving Response

Keith Williams' book on behavioural marketing contains a brief description of the scientific method and experimental technique. Just to restate what you might already have learned in biology class, here is an even briefer description:

To run an experiment, you split your subjects into two groups – a control and an experimental group. Then you try to cancel the effects of all but two variables. These are the independent and the dependent variables which, if your experiment works, begin to look like cause and effect.

For instance, to find out what it takes to change someone's opinion, behavioural marketers sat their subjects down to surveys, then showed them arguments, then surveyed again. Then they compared the changes in opinion after the different types of arguments. In this way, they were able to determine just what it takes to dislodge someone's opinion.

Or, in another example, the Harvard Business School runs something called the Mind of the Market laboratory. Psychologist Stephen Kosslyn and his team use positron emission tomography (PET) scans to map out which parts of the brain are stimulated by different types of consumer experience. Subjects in a study done for an automobile manufacturer listened to descriptions of car show rooms – one dirty with rude staff, one welcoming with friendly staff and one about average. The scans revealed what parts of each subject's brain were stimulated by pleasant and unpleasant details. As a result, the manufacturer redesigned their showrooms and other large companies such as Coca Cola, General Mills and Procter & Gamble have signed up to do their own studies.

Every year, hundreds of psychological experiments are conducted, building on a century of human behavioural theory. And increasingly, the people running them have been marketing or public relations firms, working to figure out what makes you think a certain way, live a certain way, or identify with certain products. Again, no one is dabbling. The firms in question hire real behavioural scientists to advise real statisticians and real computer scientists.

Interactive television will make their work a thousand times easier. A friend, a guide, an interactive companion – there are so many ways to describe the new relationship people will have with their televisions. But when they talk to each other, people in the industry turn to the language of lab rats and salivating dogs. Here Robin Melvyn of NTL speaks with the new vocabulary of home entertainment:

"You have to create some control group testing, in effect throw people some placebos. So if we're trying to increase their spend, or increase their usage or increase their customer satisfaction scores, we'll take one group and split it down the middle and expose it to two separate batches of data presentation."

To understand why behavioural experiments run on interactive televisions are so important, consider two difficulties facing anyone conducting such experiments.

The first difficulty is the size of sample. A worthwhile study of personality requires hundreds or thousands of subjects. Usually researchers must settle for a small number of people, whom they choose to be as representative as possible of the entire population.

The second difficulty is testing environment. It must be artificial, in as much as it can be controlled and measured. On the other hand, people may not respond naturally to any environment that is not their own, where they spend most of their lives. Usually researchers must compromise between intimacy and control.

A tool which has proved useful in overcoming these difficulties is the personal computer. It can be placed in a wide variety of situations, and people are increasingly comfortable using them.

The machine itself does the following useful things:

- Presents information in different formats
- Presents more than one activity at a time
- Presents information using different sounds, different colours, or an entire virtual environment, a desk top or virtual room for instance.
- Records keyed responses, the timing of keystrokes, clicks on a screen and users' movements in and around virtual space.

These features allow a PC to create a rich, but tightly controlled environment that can measure and respond to a subject's behaviour. They also make clear why interactive TV will be so powerful. It creates experimental conditions in the home. As with in any experiment, the whole point of your TV gathering information about you is to close a loop of stimulus, measurement and response. From now on, this loop is where all television viewers will live, as the people running the experiments try out different dependent and independent variables.

Why not have a go in the driver's seat? Imagine yourself in control of an interactive television company's direct marketing department. Come on, let's empower those viewers!:

Step One: Identify a large pool of subjects that are somehow the same. Maybe they all live in the same area, or they live in different areas, but all share the same profile. For instance, you might use collaborative filtering to identify a group which has a certain percent likelihood of living the same lifestyle or holding the same opinions.

Step Two: Pick your dependent variable. This is the behaviour you want to create. What are you trying to make the viewer do?

Buy something?

Watch more TV?

Click more ads?

Spend more money?

Hold a different opinion?

Let's say you are trying to get people to sterilise themselves. You will have to build into your experiment ways to measure your results. Maybe, behind the scenes, you are in a position to match your subscriber list to credit card payments at the local clinic. But more accurate for now would probably just be a button on the screen marked "Tell me more about responsible parenting!"

Step Three: Pick your independent variable. This is a television programming variable you can change for each experimental group. You could show each group a different commercial where little characters act out scenes.

Step Four: Run the experiment. Break down your pool of subjects into 10 groups. Group A is the control, and just sees the animated characters making small talk. In the episode shown to group B, Chachi, who has just decided to have another child, is hit by a bus. Group C might see Chachi driven to gambling by the pressure of caring for his large family, and group D might see Maria, who has been sterilised, get a promotion at her job... and so on.

Step Five: Take measurements. Which group showed the most interest? Let's say it was group F, who saw Chachi break down in tears after losing his job and being unable to feed his many children. You now have one successful generation of results. Let's move on to the next.

Step Six: Get a new pool of households. Choose people who fit the same profile you tested before. This time, all your groups will see the commercial where Chachi breaks down in tears. But each will be offered a different way to respond. Some will be offered a button marked "send me a brochure". Some will be offered a form to book a sterilisation right away. Others will be offered an immediate phone consultation with a family advisor (who will suggest sterilisation). And so on.

All together, there are three important elements that will make up direct marketing on interactive television:

- Viewer profiles
- Programming variables
- Desired behaviours

By moving from one generation of subjects to another, each time trying new values in one of these three variables, you can gradually approach the perfect commercial to make a particular type of viewer do a particular desired behaviour.

This scientific approach to changing the way people think and act is not new.

"Direct marketers have been doing that for a long time anyway," says Howard Hughes of NTL. They will start with a set package to mail or message to say, a set group of consumers to address or telephone, and their method of consumer response. After a while, they work out a normal response rate to use as a benchmark. "Once in a while," says Hughes, "they will test a different creative with a small group, and if it turns out to be a lot bigger, a lot better result than what their standard is, then they'll run with that creative across the whole group."

Direct marketing has always been like the board game Cluedo (called Clue in America). The perfect junk mail campaign is hidden, and to find it the marketers stand in different rooms on the board, calling out what they think it might be. "I think it's the yellow pamphlet mailed to lower middle-class families, asking them to call our toll-free number". They could move systematically from one room to another, eliminating any mailings that didn't work. But, as in the board game, that strategy might alert their competitors and customers. So they have to disguise their intentions.

The real problem is time. Each turn in this game takes weeks or months. For each turn, a company might have to design new material, do another mailing, await the results, enter the results, analyse what can be changed, run surveys or focus groups asking people about the new and old designs, and then do more mailings. Telephone calls are more flexible, but cost more per person reached.

"Even that has a very slow cycle," says Howard Hughes, "and it's very expensive. On the electronic medium it's not. The turnaround time is going to be a couple of days when it used to be six months."

Interactive television will make entire direct marketing campaigns as easy to do as buying a classified ad in a newspaper. It means more variables can be tested, more groups can be targeted for less money, and more people who don't respond to one message can be shown something else. As the cycles of trial and error turn more quickly, advertisers can break their messages down into smaller and smaller segments, approaching the ideal segment of one. Marketers can stop thinking in terms of individual campaigns and treat the entire system as a single engine.

Control of that engine will increasingly be automated. Once again, as computing power is hooked into every home by interactive television, data will find data. Adaptive systems can be used to control the entire process of elimination described above. It is learning process, ideally suited to the systems already used to gather data.

"I don't think they've really let neural network technology loose on some of these things," says Robin Melvyn of NTL, "which I know it's capable of, being sort of let out of the box. It can go for a walk by its own."

A good example of how such systems work is a robot created at the University of Sussex. Looking like a toy car with an insect's head carrying a microchip, the robot was placed in a large square box and went crashing into walls. Its software was told to avoid the walls, but not told how.

So it tried different things, observed the results, looked favourably on anything that worked and began to distrust anything which led to a crash against the walls. To speed the learning process, its microchip was put into a PC and a virtual robot did weeks' worth of driving around a virtual box in just a few hours. When the chip was put back in the robot, it drove in a neat square, hitting nothing.

Now, who programmed the robot? Nobody. It learned how to drive on its own. How did it do that? It just kept trying things, always measuring its progress and keeping a note of which actions worked and which didn't. That is how any learning or adaptive system works, and that is how software based on such systems will run interactive television.

It is a matter of pride and excitement to people like Howard Hughes that a selection of commercials and groups of viewers can be fed into this system and, after a few days, out come the sales!

This use of artificial intelligence is similar to the clustering techniques described in the last chapter. But instead of clustering products together around viewers, the software will cluster three things: desired behaviours, viewer profiles and television programming variables. The software is no longer just asking "who buys what?", but "what techniques will get who to buy or do what at what times?"

All those ads, services and games, all those special prices and last chance offers can be tested and co-ordinated for maximum effectiveness, automatically. Whatever your weakness, for long nights on the couch or impulse purchases on plastic, your television will find and exploit them. When used with behavioural marketing techniques, these adaptive systems will fight a non-stop battle of psychological warfare with viewers and their families.

The behavioural marketing theory will be essential, according to Pat Dade. In marked contrast to empiricists like Howard Hughes of NTL, Dade rejects the idea that artificial intelligence, left to itself, could find programming variables that get the required results.

"That's your monkeys trying to type Shakespeare," he says "Because if you don't have a theory, if you don't have a hypothesis to test, then you're not going to get anywhere."

In choosing a theory to work from, Dade typically stresses the importance of empathy with viewers: "You need a high level one that says these are people and not collections of behaviours... Spend your time on understanding how they see themselves and then we can look at the type of variables that are going to influence them. But if you don't put into the mix how they see themselves, well, there's more stars in the universe than there are variables in one 30 second TV spot."

Dade uses the trial and error methods of direct marketers. He's happy to use data mining and adaptive systems. But notice how important it is for anyone using these techniques to correctly define their groups of viewers, programming variables and desired behaviours. For Dade, and theorists like him, these definitions are always the starting place, where an understanding of human beings must be introduced. He would not trust a computer to make up its own system of content codes, and, in step one of the process above, his pool of viewers to test would always be chosen from his psychographic profiles of the population.

Mark Albert, business development director at Alto has called "cracking personality in real time" the "ideal goal" of behavioural marketing, but only in the context of warning that it wouldn't happen for a long time. However, cracking personality in real time is not necessary. Companies like Synergy can go away and crack personality outside real time.

Dade has access to his value groups, samples of people who have volunteered to try any product, answer any question and take part in any discussion. Just as researchers at the University of Sussex were able hurry their robot's learning by sending its software to explore a virtual box, so Synergy can link tests done on unsuspecting viewers to experiments done in person with willing volunteers.

Winston Smith might see one commercial for Cheese Grenades™ followed the next week by another. But in between, a

---

There's more to life than buying things.

Your TV will also be learning how to make you think things or do things. For example, the TV must always be selling itself. And though data mining software, running through your data, will bring up its own suggestions for better profitability, here are a few square boxes that your TV will probably be invited to run around:

What would a television have to do to keep you watching longer?

Keeping you glued to the set is the most important behaviour your TV provider will want to influence. Television controllers, who create a channel's line-up of entertainment, never think in terms of shows. They have always worked with your leisure hours as a single block, running from dinner to bedtime. So, for instance, they run popular comedies or dramas, their "bankers", early in the evening, because after they are finished, most people will just keep watching. American networks are now "going seamless". That is, they start a new show as soon as the last one ended. This way they don't lose anyone at the commercial break. And everyone is familiar with the way commercials pile up at the end of a programme, when you have been hooked on the plot.

Broadcasters now have software to pick through every moment of a programme to determine just when viewing figures go up or down. Using this information, they can deduce which parts of TV programmes have been losing people – to the kitchen, the bathroom, or other channels.

"Obviously," says Howard Hughes, "for a television provider it's important to get people watching, improve ratings and offer that to advertisers. All this is about changing habits."

All these techniques evolved with little knowledge of what viewers were doing in their homes. What new techniques might be available when every button you click is recorded?

group of people who think like Winston might have been shown, and spent a long time discussing, many other versions. Using this learning approach also allows the creation of better and better telegraphic signatures that bind Winston to his value group. It is important to understand the difference between a group of subjects in a psychological study and Pat Dade's use of his value groups. It is the same difference that exists between a psychologist's PC and any of the millions of digital television

Let's say Winston Smith gets sleepy and turns off his television at 10 o'clock every night. That information will be easily available to the SpyTV cable company, who then work out a way to keep him watching another half hour longer. Tonight, at 9:45, just as the movie Winston is watching is about to end, his TV set might invite him to see another movie by his favourite director.

Maybe Winston ignores the offer and goes to bed. But if the TV provider makes him similar offers every night for a week, and one of those nights he stays up, then the broadcaster has managed to capture another hour or two hours of Winston's free time. After a year of this, when Winston's average bedtime has moved to 10:30, the television can start making him offers at 10:15. What gets offered will depend on what worked and didn't work this time.

What would get you more involved with a programme?

Data mining software will help the marketing department establish patterns of involvement in all of your viewing, from which to work backwards, towards the show you just can't turn off. You'll see every episode, buy the tee shirt and join in the chat at the website.

How much advertising will you watch? And other improved telegraphics

What time of day do you watch the most TV? When are you the most impatient? When are you happy to sit through commercials? What types of viewers are most likely to click on a certain type of advertising? What kind of clicking around channels is most likely to be yours, and not your husband's?

"One of the things we can observe," says Hughes, "is that some groups of people don't like being pestered. Their tolerance for a direct approach is very low and if you hit them too directly with stuff, they turn off. So maybe you have to redirect them to an area where the advertising is built in more subtly, less aggressively."

receivers in production. This difference is the one between experimental and applied science.

One box runs experiments on samples to test theories about the general population. The other box uses established theory to observe and affect its subject directly. Its use of the scientific method does not run "experiments" at all, but "applications".

When an interactive TV set modifies or reinforces existing behaviour, it is not conducting experiments any more than a thermostat could be said to conduct experiments on the temperature of a room.

TV viewers are themselves the general population, in their natural environment. And by putting a computer into every single home, television providers will have done more than set up a nice experiment – they will have created a machine. It has been designed, from the start, to offer control..

Time Again

Marketers no longer have to scream "Buy This!" and hope they catch you on the way to the supermarket. They now have time on their side. Any set of experiments or incentives can be spread out through weeks and years, getting your attention, introducing new attitudes, changing your beliefs and encouraging new behaviours.

Right now, as a consumer, you move through a stream of branding and advertising messages. In the future, you will be nudged along your own stream, with every company monitoring your progress through predefined stages of involvement with their brands. When speakers at the Family Power '99™ conference talk about "child psyche-based ideation and age segmentation integration", they mean that as each child grows, he or she will be given different messages.

When launching a new product, for instance, marketers have always been forced to appeal to "the market" and speak in terms of "public image" or "brand visibility". But they've always known that the market was just millions of individuals, brand visibility was just the sum of their contacts with the brand, public image was just the sum of what they understood and sales were just the last in a chain of events that took place inside each house.

With interactive TV, marketers can now think in terms of millions of launches inside millions of homes. So instead of using one launch message, or even a message designed to prepare the public, followed by an announcement, marketers can now create one or more multi-stage campaigns for each household.

Before the launch, a marketer can research the available viewer profiles and each household's current telegraphic behaviour. He can put the final touches on a selection of campaigns, each to be introduced in stages.

The marketer can then prepare each household, or person within a household, to receive the launch message. Any attitudes against the message would be targeted for weakening. Any fears a consumer has about trying something new would be soothed. At this stage, product placement and planted news items would be especially useful. Just as is done now, companies will want to generate discussion of the product and the brand. But instead of planting their stories in the press and hoping for the best, they will be able to create and monitor public awareness on a house by house basis. A company or government could begin its preparatory work and launch in any household only when it showed it was ready to buy.

Then each home could be hit with its own, customised launch. People new to the product might be shown pictures of people using the product. People new to the brand might be encouraged to switch from the product they use now. When the first group is familiar with the product, they could be offered a free sample. The second group could be offered branded services or a discount.

By measuring viewer response in clicks and sales, the campaign can be designed to turn up the volume only as fast as people are willing to accept. After the launch, the marketer could run another set of ads, encouraging satisfied customers to tell friends and offering people who didn't buy a reason to stay in touch. The launch of a product is only one event in time that marketers prepare for, execute and follow up. Other events might be the launch of a competitor's product, the launch of a government policy, or a national election.

Then of course there are the events in your life. Jonathan Plowden Roberts of the Database Group has talked of event driven marketing and of marketers' desire to know when you plan to buy a car or have a child. Interactive TV will soon observe each of these events, helping you prepare, helping you through the big day, and then checking up afterwards to see that everything is all right. Many people will, no doubt, find this reassuring. Others will perhaps remember a time when such information was nobody's business but their own.

Marketers will have to come to grips with their new role as everyone's guardian angels. Like fairy godmothers, the people who make interactive TV will be able to grant wishes and dole out punishments. So that "The Methodology" used to prod soap opera viewers into literacy or family planning can now be played out for real, with some viewers offered prizes while others miss out. If these groups of people interact, then the TV can orchestrate its own social network soap opera.

Friends Again

How many bars of soap do you have to sell to ten of your friends to buy a communications satellite? The multi-level marketing company Amway would know, because they've shot one into space. Last year this company made billions of dollars, most of it from people who sold Amway products to people they knew. This is one example of the new marketing. In the future, any marketing campaign will operate less like a movie premiere or hit record, and more like an election drive or a religious cult.

"Develop friends of your brand" writes Bernadette Tracy, president of NetSmart in her essay Beyond Branding to Bonding. "Make sure you give visitors a truly motivating reason to return and to tell others." This common sense advice illustrates just how the work of advertisers is about to change. Just as interactive TV encourages them to use the dimension of time, so they will now move through networks of friends, acquaintances and families. Instead of pushing a message, the marketers of tomorrow will be gathering and mobilising groups of supporters.

Interactive television will allow them to accomplish this on a mass scale. Who watches programmes about new technology and is the first to buy any new gizmo? These people are the all-important "early adopters", and interactive television will be able to make special offers to the early adopters you know. What if that friend of yours who always has the latest thing buys a certain brand of gadget? Chances are, he'll recommend it to you when you look into buying something similar.

What if all the top executives at your company were offered a deal on a certain brand of clothing, car or handheld computer? Would you feel left out? What if everyone on the football team at your school were wearing the same running shoes? Or what if all the well-off kids in your class had been offered a deal on a brand of bicycle or wristwatch? How would you feel then?

Any club, team or social group you belong to can be targeted this same way. Each one will have its own group dynamics, its own leaders and followers. Sales will go to the company with the best information and the best strategy for playing members of the group off against each other.

And the great thing about interactive TV is its ability to sell with discretion. Whether or not a marketer mentions other people is up to him. Sometimes, it may be prudent not to mention other people and thereby allow awareness of the product to build in the group without anyone noticing the concentrated sales effort. Later, it may be useful to purposely tie customers together, building on the identity they share as members of the group. Everyone in an office can be offered a special price product or service, perhaps on the invitation of one person, who acts as contact. Meanwhile, that contact and a smaller, select group, can be offered their own incentives to try something else.

These marketing techniques are as old as buying and selling. They simply require some understanding of how a group gets information, absorbs change and makes decisions. In other words, that group's psychology. Interactive TV allows the creation of marketing campaigns targeted directly at the psychographic profile of an organisation.

And as mentioned before, the one informal involuntary group to which everyone belongs is the household, usually a family. No social unit has been studied so long in such detail. Only now, with interactive television will marketers play a full role inside homes, where viewers and their families interact. Every family will fit a profile and every family will show signs of where they stand in a cycle of changes and purchases. What an interactive TV set can then do is manage the information that different family members have and, to some extent, influence a set of interactions.

Working slowly, carefully, building coalitions of support, isolating opponents – it could be said this is how any salesman or politician has done his work for hundreds of years, before television. But now he doesn't need to ring the doorbell or stick his foot inside, he will live with us, in various rooms of the house, giving customised pitches to each person who lives there.

Imagine: the television in Winston Jr's room could offer him a video game in which he races the advertiser's new model car, the Victory, against his dad's old banger. Downstairs, Winston is watching the headlines. It seems that his car did badly in some safety tests. By coincidence, a commercial comes on for the Victory, featuring a father and son driving together. Just then, Junior comes in. He is pleasantly surprised.

Interactive television will even be able to influence self-selected, informal groups, otherwise known as friends. It will offer them services: chat rooms, video games, online beepers, mail lists and ordinary email. All can all be analysed to produce lists of people who keep in regular contact. Whether they are used this way depends on the law and people's willingness to put up with it. But even when groups of friends cannot be identified, they can be created. Such a strategy is clearly visible on the internet where people reaching out to their "like minded peers" come back with a fistful of branding.

In 1998, the advertising giant Saatchi & Saatchi sent psychologists and cultural anthropologists into dozens of online chat rooms. Their conclusions about people who use these virtual "third places" as if they were coffee shops and bars were offered in an essay titled "A Fly on the Virtual Wall: Cybercommunities Observed."

The report's author, Myra Stark, describes how each of these personal, informal meetings can be turned into the a powerful branding exercise. She advises marketers to create, sponsor or underwrite such communities so that "the brand communication is the community". She continues: "The intense loyalty of members to their cybercommunities is exactly what the marketer needs to build long-term relationships between consumers and brands."

Her work followed an article titled "The Real Power of Online Communities" in the Harvard Business Review, which made the same point:

"By creating strong online communities, businesses will be able to build consumer loyalty to a degree that today's marketers can only dream of and, in turn, generate strong economic returns."

Anthony Lilley of Magic Lantern, a producer of interactive television programmes, told the interactive advertising conference in London: "television is really about communities of potential buyers" and that a good TV show could build those communities. "How does it really work?" he asked, and behind him was projected the one word in large letters: "DATABASES".

An organisation that creates and therefore owns such an online group is in a position to monitor and even censor what participants contribute. Participants benefit from this arrangement only to the extent that they support the aims of the organisation which owns the group – Shell oil executives in a news group owned by Shell for instance, or environmentalists in a news group owned by Greenpeace.

More difficult to understand has been the participation of thousands of people in internet forums about the environment, sponsored by Shell. And that is on the internet, where any of the participants could easily have started his or her own discussion. On the costly, tightly controlled medium of interactive television, online communities run by public relations departments will be the norm. Meanwhile, the organisations that own the databases behind these websites will be in a good position to do their own imitation grass-roots networking.

Imagine a PR disaster scenario for any government or company. Just as they prepare now, with entire "dark" websites ready to mount at a moment's notice, interactive televisions across the country would broadcast material putting the organisation's point of view. Televison providers would be in a good position to guess who had and had not heard about the disaster, and software could make snap decisions about how to break the news or answer criticisms, depending on what viewers already knew. Likely supporters of the organisation could be mobilised, likely waverers could be won over and likely opponents could be deliberately confused or pacified in some way.

How these groups of people then interact on the streets, in the work place and in the home can all, to some extent, have been influenced and even orchestrated by the organisation's public relations office. This is the marketing, the advertising and the politics of the future.

Fun

by Deirdre Devers

INTERACTIVE TELEVISION has been sold as opening up a new world to children. When people said the same of the internet, the meaning of the phrase was simple – the bodies who own the airwaves lost control of a medium that let everyone have their say. Large amounts of information and communication become freely available from, and moves between, ordinary people from all over. And the world which was opened up was not new or virtual at all. It was our own.

The virtual worlds came later, especially after the creation of the world wide web. By switching emphasis from the information people exchange to the clicking they do to get it, many games, works of fiction, and on-screen "hangouts" were created. What defines these online places is their element of control. Visitors have control of what happens within an unreal "space", the design of which is in total control of a designer. They are not communications with Earth, but an alternative to it, measured in users' hours of enjoyment and whatever else their designers have in mind.

For a number of reasons, it is these virtual worlds that have attracted the interest and sponsorship of broadcasters and marketers. They have gone on to change how people think of the internet and they have begun to change how people behave in the real world.

On interactive television, such virtual worlds, usually created by ad agencies, will be the only ones on offer. And the people for whom most of them have been designed are children, those earliest of early adopters of new technology. To see how everyone will live with interactive television, it is worth examining these worlds that the next generation of interactive consumers already inhabit.

The first kid on the block to get interactive television has reason to be excited. He can check the Pokemon website to see when the next Pokemon GameBoy competition is coming to the local mall while downloading a voucher for £3 off Pokemon accessories. He pushes buttons and the television responds to his input by navigating according to the programmer's digital architecture. He feels good that he is able to do something on his own with this new, knowing electronic device.

His mother feel secure knowing that their child can spend leisure time tuned in to interactive children's programming which encourages him to learn and participate. She feels reassured that her child can take what he has learned from his favourite educational interactive programming, chat about what he has learned in "kids-only" chat rooms, or play video games (based on his favourite programmes) in real time with other children across the country or around the world.

For both mother and child, it is a great improvement over passive television viewing. But the relief they feel, and their need for increasingly sophisticated entertainment technology are themselves a new phenomenon. Any virtual world must take place inside a real one, most frequently a child's bedroom. And it is there, in that room, that interactive media desires, advertisers, sociologists, doctors and, finally, parents are turning their full attention. What is important about any interactive media is not what is presented on the screen, but what goes on around it.

"Families have become more fragmented," says Matthew Timms of Two Way TV, "We've found that most of the families that we were talking to tended to have three or more TVs in their home and everybody would go off and watch their own programs on their own TVs; you know there's more channels, more choice."

As Timms demonstrates, children are increasingly seen as sophisticated consumers of their own media experiences, making their own decisions about what they watch and how they interact with machines. But a five year, Europe-wide study of children has recently questioned whether children actually have the choices they want.

In Britain, Dr. Sonia Livingstone of the London School of Economics has described a process she observed from interviews with children at home whereby nervous parents keep children inside from fear of crime and traffic. To avoid arguments and make up for the loss of freedom, parents buy their children entertainment technology to explore. So computers and televisions are not the first choice of these supposedly sophisticated young media consumers. Repeatedly, what children told Livingstone they wanted most was the freedom to go outside and be with friends. A study in Zurich went further, describing children as either "free range" or "battery". The "battery" children were poorly socialised, aggressive and prone to depression.

The excitement of exploring virtual worlds is being offered to children not in addition to, but in place of something. Only now are people beginning to count the real world cost of virtual convenience. Dr. Anthony Underwood is a pediatrician in Australia who has been studying the effect of television on children's imaginations.

"When a child comes into my surgery who watches a lot of television, I can tell," says Underwood, and describes what happens when such a child is offered some blocks to play with. "The child will not know how to play with them. He'll wait for instructions or ask what they do."

To doctors or parents, news of children with impaired imaginations trapped in their bedrooms is troubling. But, by what is hopefully just a coincidence, it is nothing but good news for people whose livelihoods depend on a captive, unquestioning audience. Virtual worlds, full of children with nowhere else to go, are a marketing man's dream.

Once again, it boils down to control. The things a child learns on screen, he applies to his real life. Experiences in cyberspace influence behaviour and social conduct in the real world. While offering exploration in a box, the makers of television have always known that their real business depends on what goes on outside it – the very same living room, home, family, friends and neighbourhood streets that are supposedly so boring and unsafe. The symmetrical relationship of the virtual place to the real place is designed to facilitate control over individual and household spending.

The need for such control is described by Daniel Bobruff of the branded video games designer Microtime Media:

"The advertiser now cannot just rely on targeting audiences when he finds it and where he finds it," says Bobruff. "That was the days of old. And it was very easy... We were following audiences. Today we have to help form them."

The strategy of control, whereby interactive media influences children's lives as consumers, has these three components: physical proximity, emotional engagement and occupation of creative imagination.

Keep 'Em In

It is important for marketers that children remain glued to the set, or that the set hangs glued to them. Broadcasters claim that watching television is only one activity out of many available to a healthy child. But when they speak to each other in the trade press, or when ABC spends millions of dollars on a "TV is Good" campaign, it becomes clear that they are very worried about those other things children could be doing, away from the screen. And they make it their business to edge those other activities out of the picture.

Physical proximity to media has always been crucial to broadcasters, who must fill any screen with a flickering stream of images and sounds known as "bit changes". They are what elicit, maintain and terminate the viewer's attention. The goal is to produce what is known as "attentional inertia", whereby the longer a child viewer continues to look at a television, the more likely it is that the child will continue to do so.

The importance of this state becomes obvious when you consider that it has also been shown to work in reverse: the longer since a child has looked at a television screen (because of doing something else for example) the less likely it is that he or she will return. Watching and not watching are both habit forming, which is why interactivity is so important. The television interface, through the stratagem of interactivity attempts to keep users watching and playing through their involvement. Matthew Timms describes the success they've had at Two Way TV:

"We'll get a lot of people who like playing games staying in to watch [an interactive] show instead of going and doing something else. We've shown that if people can join in, they're more likely to watch the show."

As is already done on the internet, interactivity allows the use of a meeting place or hangout metaphor, meant to take the place of the tree houses or street corners that are now off limits. The Kellogg's Club House™ web page welcomes young users with the following meticulously researched kidspeak:

"Hey there Cyberslackers, you've made it to Kellogg's Clubhouse™, the hottest stop for the hippest Web hopper... Looking for some household hype? Then eyeball these Awesome Activities, or send a stylin cybersurprise with Kellogg's™ E-cards."

Nobody is actually at this website, except illustrations of Snap, Crackle and Pop reading the letters they've been sent. The site should probably provide some animation quickly if it is to keep up with the proliferation of club houses, secret clubs, hideaways and virtual soda shops crowding the web with various well-drawn, well-researched non-entities. Children are willing to join in these simple imitations of companionship because, looking around their own houses, they have little choice.

Almost like playing with a real friend, the virtual world is a shielded and private place for expression, in which parents are rarely involved. Almost like playing outside, a child is given a sense of power by exerting control over characters on the screen. A virtual world will also offer incentives for returning, calling the child by his or her name, or offering rewards such as vouchers. "For instance," says Matthew Timms of Two Way TV, "in a pre-school, three or four year old type of programme, we run a recognition game so that whenever a particular character runs on screen you press a button and you get a reward for having seen it happen." The virtual world also provides for a child's real life needs without the responsibilities or social demands of real life. In the Kellogg's Clubhouse™, a child isn't chastised or bullied or told off by teachers. It's a great benefit to the growing number of children who, for some reason, now suffer from shyness.

Digital technology not only improves the power and attractiveness of a virtual hang out, it allows the advertising content of the virtual hangout, and any ersatz relationships created therein, to be reproduced in new places on new media. Everything from refrigerators to mobile phones are gaining screens and links to broadcast or narrowcast content to become "thin client" devices, of which the interactive television is just the most visible example.

Scott Randall is CEO of Brand Games, a creator of advertising driven video games in New York. He told attendees at Kid Power '99 in London "Over the years, youth marketers have gone to great expense to use the fantasy power of images to create a world for their brand – but then what? Until now, they've been unable to extend and sustain this world into the daily lives of their consumers."

Now, even when a child moves away from the TV set, the clubhouse can follow him. Here is some of the promotional copy for the philosophy Randall has been selling on the conference circuit:

"Discover how to 'surround' your consumers with your brand and establish relationships with them. Convergence Marketing™: BrandGames' strategy for developing sustainable relationships with today's digital consumers by layering and linking convergent advertiser-funded programming throughout their daily experience."

The approach is more ambitious than simply advertising everywhere a company can afford to advertise. The surrounding Randall describes here is less like music in an airport and more like the action of sheep dogs herding their flock:

"Create this unbelievable animated world around your brand mascot. Put it on TV – it's broadband, it's passive, kids get to know the characters' personalities – Oh Wow! Now the kids are all excited. Now put that world on a video game, so you've maintained the rich media experience, but now you've added interactivity to it. So now your kids are playing in that world: good. Okay, now over to the internet, and there's a website that allows you to manage either a merchandising operation, a call centre, tech support or whatever."

This effort, to have children play in the worlds of a marketing man's invention, has been given an impressive boost by the invention of interactive dolls tied to, and controlled by television programmes. Consider, for instance, Microsoft's interactive Actimates® Barney toy, which remains activated by the programme only as long as it stays within a 15 foot radius of the television. Even away from the television, interactive Teletubby Tinky Winky performs animatronic movements and speaks 20 different phrases As the child moves from one real place to another, he or she remains within the world of the brand mascot. Such toys metaphorically corral children within an advertisement, regardless where the child moves in their physical space. The child's attention is maintained.

But, as Randall points out, the crucial beginning of the process is a relationship between the child and a branded character, begun on the television screen. This emotional engagement will become more important as interactive techniques allow branded characters to do more, and become closer friends to young viewers.

Keep 'Em Close

The anthropomorphism of interactive toys through convergence technologies has been making a big splash at toy fairs, with the best selling toys enjoying the familiarity provided by a previous life on the TV screen. An interactive Barney doll can not only tell its owner when it's time to wake up, but accompanies them to the living room to "interact" with the Barney programme and chime affirmations to the child such as, "I like watching TV with you."

Erik Strommen is the chief content developer for Microsoft's Actimates, and a developmental psychologist by training. 'These dolls," he says "are treated by children as if they are another person. They talk back to them, they laugh at their jokes. The dolls respond in a way that a good friend and a good learning partner would respond – they praise their successes, offer hints when you want them, that kind of thing.'

Jim Withers of Koplar Interactive Systems International makes similar claims: "Well, you're watching with a friend all of a sudden." He describes an interactive toy his company has helped create:

"It's a Pokemon [interactive] toy that interacts directly with [the child]. Something happens on TV and the Pokemon says to the little guy who's watching, 'Wasn't that fun Kaylie?' and uses the viewers name in response. That's because when you buy the Pokemon toy, the parent programs it to know the kids name... kids think it's magic."

Games and electronic toys are, in many ways, the cutting edge of man-machine interface. And, rather than just accepting instructions from a user, today's computers guide users in different directions. Call it "user friendliness" or call it "user control", but entire conferences have been held on the subject. Speaking at the CHI 99 Computer Interaction Conference in Pittsburgh, B.J. Fogg of Stanford's Persuasive Technology Laboratory discussed the role that interactive toys like Barney might someday play inside the family. He envisioned a time when interactive dolls could "sense" when there was a fast-food restaurant within it's proximity and could murmur "Mmm, I smell french fries. I'm hungry – aren't you?"

"It's really sobering and instructive to study the persuasive potential of technology" says Fogg, "You can't underestimate the power of a toy."

This power to persuade is exactly what Scott Randall of Brand Games is paid to wield for his clients. Here he describes the challenge following up that initial, magical introduction:

"To us," says Randall, "all this stuff is new. The kids are open books. You tell the kid that he should be able to interact with the character, he goes 'Okay, cool.'... I see this all the time. We test stuff with kids and expect them to go 'Wow, that's cool!' They go 'Okay. So now that he talks to me, what do I do?'"

Screen or toy, regardless of age, a child's interaction with animated characters is always guided by an ulterior motive of influence over the child's real life. Emotional engagement is not just an emotional state; it is a behaviour, a commitment on the part of the child to continue interacting. Promotional copy for Microsoft's Actimates® Barney doll reassures parents that it is "a viewing buddy" and "helps children become more involved with the program". And the people who send instructions to these toys in peoples' homes have begun to answer this question, "What do I do?" Their instructions are ultimately aimed at the young user.

Jim Withers of Koplar Interactive makes clear what is achieved when a child forms an attachment to his magical toys: "That's the killer application. If you can find something that a kid walks away from the show saying, 'That is an additional reason for me to wanna watch the show tomorrow.'"

The interactivity developed for Barney, which spills over into a child's non-media life, is nothing like having a real friend. The love and sense of security that a character or toy provides is transferred to a product or service. But for the toy's designer, it represents a success. An empathetic impression through emotional attachment has been made on the child, and it transfers to the brand.

"Play affects empathy," says Christian Fernandez, director of sales and marketing at Static 2358 Limited, an interactive advertising producer. "Whenever you try to build the brand with a game, you turn the brand into the hero of the game and get some kind of empathy." This is why the most effective ads are ones in which the child recognises some part of themselves in the brand personality or character because this arouses the child's actual feelings. Tony Schwartz (1973) calls this strategy "resonance".

Such emotional attachment is not made at random. Advising the advertising and broadcast industries, there is a new breed of "character consultants", whose job it is to marry the emotional needs of children to the business objectives of marketers. Dan Acuff is a character consultant to companies such as Disney and M&M/Mars. His work draws on Maslow to create the following five ways in which children identify with any character:

- Nurture me / I nurture it
- It is like me
- Emulation
- Entertainment
- Villains – I'm not like that.

This list springs from another list of 10 needs for kids and adults. Any television character or television controlled doll must provide the following:

- Stimulation/New levels of stimulation
- Love
- Acceptance
- Success
- Reality
- Control
- Power
- Release or the letting go of emotion
- Safety
- Growth

These needs are important psychosocial motivators. Raising children under constant parental supervision in the home, with diminished social connections to neighbours or friends, parents are forced to improvise new ways to meet these needs. When they are no longer able to improvise, marketers like Acuff, and his clients, are stepping in to offer interactive solutions from a box. Increasingly, interactive television and the internet are being called on to offer substitutes for real life friends and experiences.

Children in the future will have access to a wide selection of conversations with machines. Characters that speak and act with artificial intelligence will elicit psychological responses akin to social relationships in the real world. So, for instance, a child might have real conversations with a Barney toy on screen in the day at school and in bed at night. No doubt all such services will carry notices to parents, reassuring them that the simulated personalities have been designed through testing on real children, under the supervision of specialists.

Much better are the services that involve other children in a virtual chat room. But, unlike face to face conversation in a park or school yard, the entire meeting takes place under the auspices of, and around the subject of a particular brand. So most children will be meeting to get tips on playing a game, or acquiring a particular Pokemon character. Interactions may be friendly, but there are few opportunities for, or challenges requiring real friendship.

However realistic they become, all these services in the virtual world will allow children to avoid the intricacies and unpleasantness of real human interaction. They are a child's own, composed only of things the child likes and likes doing. Meanwhile, the entire situation is moderated by adults who work for the brand.

"And there's never been," continued Scott Randall of Brand Games to the Kid Power '99 audience, "a reliable way to turn media 'impressions' into one-to-one relationships, or to service those relationships with continuity and consistency."

Ultimately, the emotional relationships offered to children will be better and better versions of one to one relationship marketing. And, as with other one to one relationships through interactive television, information will be gathered from and used to gain influence over children. Has Two Way TV, for instance, ever extracted information from children?

"Yes," says Matthew Timms, "because it comes back automatically. What we can ask people to do is put in their details of people who are actually playing there and then. Obviously you can't do too much because it's off-putting. But we can ask kids to say how old they are and what their name is and all that kind of stuff."

Internet sites have, for a long time, been asking children to complete questionnaires and online registration forms. But more important than any demographic or lifestyle data contained in their answers are the hints they give away about the games they would like to play and what kind of animated friends they might like to have. The emotional component of a child's one to one relationship with a brand is much more powerful, and useful, than any adult's.

For example, Brand Games has published a CD ROM game in which the nine General Mills cereal characters play together against any of 31 major league baseball teams. Scott Randall describes how kids relate to it:

"Well, the kid sits around playing this for 40 trillion hours and goes to the store, he's just spent 30 zillion hours with these nine characters. They're his friends. 'Ohhh, there's the guy, awww, Mommy, here's my friend, the Trix rabbit!'"

According to Randall, advertisers have been given a huge, cinematic canvass on which to tell involving, engrossing stories that hook young consumers into lasting relationships. Some are not ready for the responsibility.

"Ad guys are always acting like they want to be film makers and 'Oh, we're so restricted by 30 seconds'. But that 30 seconds saves their lives because, if they really had to tell a story, what would they do? [Some ad executives] are scared to death of interactive advertising. And it is the biggest opportunity they ever had."

Randall is one of the few advertising professionals who realises the long term importance of his work. He is preparing to take on, for his clients, the awesome responsibility of befriending or even raising children through interactive relationships.

"You have to watch it. And you have to be responsible about it. It changes the advertising game. Right now, the advertising game is just Throw Up a Message and Collect a Commission Cheque. But this whole interactivity thing has opened up a whole can of worms."

But Randall's responsibility to the children who spend zillions of hours playing with his interactive friends must always be weighed against his primary responsibility to his clients. Ultimately, for advertisers, personal relationships are a means to an end, which is a share of a child's mental environment and control over his or her consumer behaviour.

Keep 'Em Singing

The crucial question for any advertiser is this: How much does the consumer take away from an advertisement? How much of the advertisement stays in the viewer's mind, ready to trigger a sale? Studies have shown two things about television and its viewers' acceptance of advertising messages. First, it doesn't matter whether a viewer is happy or sad during a commercial. What makes the difference is their level of involvement with the programme. Second, it has been shown that viewers become more involved with a programme that offers interactive content.

"They don't spend more time [watching television]," says Matthew Timms of Two Way TV, "But they do get more out of the programmes they do watch, and they're more likely to be more likely to be more loyal once they've started playing the game.".

This is especially true in the case of children, for whom online time offers a rare emancipation from parental control. From the smallest physical motion of pushing a button to the grander movements of a child dancing and singing along with an electronic toy, interactive involvement employs the physical play of the body while the mind is actively building emotional memories through the act of playing.

Daniel Bobruff of Microtime Media says, "It's the doing of things that make people retain that information." The ability to absorb information is 40% seen, 10% heard and 50% done. Bobruff uses this as a valuable selling point to his clients. Doing is remembering. Interactive entertainment offers a powerful method of internalising the brand or character ideology. Play and the associated memories, whether in real or virtual worlds, form an emotional bond of fidelity with the object from which they have derived pleasure.

And this is why Scott Randall is not terrified of his responsibility for controlling what his animated characters will say or do for the many hours during which children play with them.

"It doesn't matter what it says, it just matters that it is. You just have to do something that catches the kids' imagination and they're on it. And you feed that pipe ... It's not where Ronald McDonald goes, it's what he stands for. What does your brand stand for? ... It doesn't really matter what the adventure is, as long as you capture the kid's imagination and that it stands for something that, for them, makes sense. And you can take that anywhere you want to take it."

In a two way process, what goes into a child's mind as experience comes out later as creative imagination. When Scott Randall talks of "catching or capturing" that process, he makes clear the real organising principle behind any interactive game or toy.

In his essay 'Limits to the Imagination: Marketing and Children's Culture', Stephen Kline describes this organising principle: "In contemporary television, marketing, rather than entertainment considerations, dominate the design of children's characters, the fictions in which they appear and hence the way children play. Play, the most important modality of childhood learning is thus colonised by marketing objectives making the imagination the organ of corporate desire."

Interactive toys and games are sold with promises that they will "set children's imaginations free." But the people who create them have very different purposes in mind. The visual and emotional imprints of play are re-activated by memories and emotions throughout a child's youth and into adulthood. When this is done successfully it is called 'layering' the consumer identifies with the brand, brand personalities or characters and so engage with the product over time. The Sesame Street characters you loved as a kid now live at the amusement park where you can take your children on vacation. What ensures your response to such marketing opportunities over the years is those characters' place in your imagination.

Not only does the visual media add characters to those available for children's imaginative play, it has, with this generation, begun to change how those imaginations work.

"Attending the movies is not a simple experience but an event re-lived through an array of colouring books, computer games and pajamas. Toys demand less imagination when the generic teddy bear is replaced by a Lion King who comes with a history by Disney," says communications researcher Norma Odom Pecora.

Stephen Kline provides a theoretical description of this difference between playing with a teddy bear and playing out a scene with a Lion King figurine:

"Play in fact has become highly ritualised – less an exploration and solidification of personal experiences and developing conceptual schema than a re-articulation of the fantasy world provided by market designers. Imaginative play has shifted one degree closer to mere imitation and assimilation."

Character consultant Acuff says it more succinctly, "You become what you pay attention to."

As more and more children turn to media consumption for entertainment and information, what they become are sophisticated media consumers, canny in their likes and dislikes, and aware of what's hot and what's not. Children as young as 24 months, are able to influence their parent's spending in an attempt to fulfil their own psychosocial needs. Parents are annoyed, but often impressed by a young child's firm decision-making ability and view the shopping cart chant of "Teletubbies, Teletubbies" as a sign of his or her maturing sense of self.

Unfortunately for the child, that is exactly true. Children are growing up savvy, but only in as much as they know what they want to buy next. Their ability to make sense of the real world outside the box of consumer culture suffers. So is there a difference between imaginative play and passive, controlled entertainment? Yes. If you listen to Scott Randall of Brand Games, it seems that one is just not worth doing.

"What," he asks, "all the couch potatoes are all of a sudden becoming Stephen Speilbergs?" Randall is dismissing the commonly heard claim that interactive media will allow viewers to control stories and share with producers a responsibility for what happens. His subject is interactive books or stories on screen. But his words are built on an assumption about the very idea that viewers want to do anything, or could do anything, other than view. Passive or interactive, it is this assumption that has, from the beginning, shaped broadcasting:

"What about the big word entertainment? Can you or I make a film that's gripping? Stephen Speilberg writes an unbelievably gripping film that has you sitting there going 'Oh my God, this guy's going to get killed!' There's film grammar involved in that, and there's music and there's guys who dedicate their lives to this. When you do a video game, you have a guy who does just the backgrounds, and a guy who does just the foregrounds, and a guy who does just the buttons. And because each one of them is a specialist, the combination makes a gripping entertainment experience. But to let that fall into the hands of just everyone – I don't know. That's kind of a weird one to me."

Leave it to the professionals. The assumption behind television, and the new toys that are "changing play" is that children depend on professionals for their imaginative experiences, and any toy which depends on a child's own "magic" to work is just deficient. The professionals have let their audience down.

Randall describes his child's disappointment when reading a book that asked him to choose the ending of an interactive story. "I sat down to read this with my kid once, he's a bright young eleven year old, and he looked at me and said 'Daddy, what is this? This is stupid.' Am I supposed to be Hemingway now? People who can put an unbelievably compelling story together and grip you… If I could do that I would be Tom Clancey. I'm not. So that one to me, again is weird."

As better and better substitutes are offered for it, the role of creative imagination in a person's life is likely to become a subject of heated debate. For some people, it will make possible the creation of a self-directed identity. For others, it will be a product, created by masters of their profession and offered to children, whose own personal identities will result from their choices as savvy consumers.

Raised in this environment, tomorrow's children will be ever more reliant on the responsible professionalism of men like Scott Randall.

Empowerment

WHAT COULD SOUND CRAZIER than someone saying "I think my TV is observing me"? What could sound crazier than someone saying "I think my TV is sending messages meant only for me"

It is very difficult to talk about this without sounding paranoid. And consider why. In the past, when someone said this, they were not just incorrect on the facts. It was likely that they were mentally ill. For them, the television was a visible manifestation of some power they feared ran the world, and had singled them out, and was lying to them, or manipulating them, or trying to control their thoughts. When someone spoke to them or something happened in their neighbourhood, a billboard going up or houses being demolished, they might have felt these actions were aimed at them, or resulted from what they had done in front of the television.

And in the past a sane person would have offered comfort. "No, you are not being singled out. No, the messages on TV are not aimed at you, or linked to anything people say on the phone. The connections you describe have been made in your own mind. No, the television is not probing you to discover your weaknesses. Even if they wanted to, no group of people could co-ordinate all these messages and events in your life. They have no reason to follow you through your life, or contact people you know. You are free."

What will sane people say in the future?

That is being decided now. As anyone in marketing knows, when you launch a product, you are seeking to define it in the consumer's mind. And as anyone in public relations knows, the battle to define issues, before the public debates them, is crucial.

This year, interactive television is being launched in countries around the world with slogans like these:

"Puts you in control…"

"Empowers the viewer…"

"Set your imagination free"

"Get involved, see what's out there!"

"The world brought to your living room!"

The goal is to find and tap into an emotion that, at times, fills even the most cynical of us – a belief in technological progress. It's a belief that has gone in and out of fashion since the industrial revolution began. Turner's painting 'Rain Steam and Speed', of a locomotive charging into darkness, has been cited as a vision of the public's emotional response to the power of the future. The man who did the citing was Andrew Curry, then head of Interactive TV at Videotron UK. Curry was describing the need to build such excitement around the launch of interactive television.

Turner's painting was done at the end of the last century. And when mass market televisions were launched in the late 1940s, using slogans almost identical to those listed above, progress was enjoying one of its periodic comebacks. The intervening years have been counted in melting reactors, skin cancers and food scares. The space flights and bomb tests of the cold war only cancelled each other out.

But that hope, that this time the scientists got it right, and we can enjoy the benefits of some new life without any drawbacks, without even having to think about the drawbacks – it's always there. Whether you dream of jet engine cars that fly or solar powered transit systems that get rid of cars forever, who hasn't been thrilled by it?

And hey, it's the millennium! Polyester is back in fashion! The people selling interactive TV sets might just catch their wave of consumer optimism. And to celebrate, they are printing long lists of goodies you will receive as soon as you have one in your house. But here is something else any marketing professional can tell you: when you are trying to sell a product that has a downside, rather than cover up the downside, just highlight the potentials.

As we've tried to show, interactive TV does have a downside. And people had better start describing it with the passion, eloquence, and especially the budget now being used to make people believe in its potentials. Without wishing to sound paranoid, here are some observations about the world that interactive TV is bringing to the comfort of your living room.

They Sell You Goodies, You Buy a Lifestyle

Like any intelligent business people, the men and women launching interactive TV are planning five to ten years ahead. The articles and interviews you read about this digital revolution will not be news to any of them. So, for instance, Neal Muranyi of the Database Group describes a period of years during which the majority of viewers do not yet have interactive TVs. Until they do, he recommends, data from the interactive minority be used as a population sample to make guesses about the rest. Then when everyone has interactive, the need for population "samples" will disappear as households are reached individually, in real time. His is then a two part, long term strategy.

Similarly, the TV industry is quietly preparing to defend itself against popular anger about its invasion of privacy. At the interactive advertising conference in London, Ron Mudge, media director of Saatchi & Saatchi warned his audience of a type of consumer called the "1984er", who would have strong emotional reservations to interactive TV. His overall advice to advertisers was to emphasise viewer control and capitalise on people's natural desire to offer their opinions.

Gadi Tirosh, Product Manager for NDS told delegates that advertisers would be in the driver's seat of interactive TV, but they must make sure people think it as a "customised service" rather than worry about privacy.

We are now in a period when issues like privacy will be deliberately ignored, while people are sold on goodies. Liz Camps is the Online Producer of a website called digitaltvreport.com. She describes the following early target markets, and how the industry should reach them:

- "Media Junkies" love TV but don't have much experience with computers. Camps advises digital TVs be put in sports bars and concludes "peer pressure will be a strong factor in enticing to purchase."
- "Fast Forwards" like gadgets, convenience and anything that makes them more competitive. Camps advises "Appeal to the Fast Forward parents' *sense of duty to the education* [emphasis hers] of their children ... Create a mystique of empowerment around the DTV device ... Do this not only with advertising, but by working time-saving gadgets into TV sitcom plots and news stories."
- "Enlightenment Seekers" are New Age Nurturers who use technology as a tool for exploring their inner mindscape. Camp quotes Forrester Research, who consider this group among the most likely to buy digital TV in the near future. She advises, without irony, "Encourage this group's longing for a "brave new world". Emphasise how DTV (digital TV) coincides with the turn of the millennium and use 'think globally, act locally' as DTV's rallying anthem."

You can just imagine the sitcom plots and news stories that Camps has in mind. Such cynical use of content to push a change in lifestyle is just a foretaste of what is to come.

Anyone with experience of the internet will find the goodies on interactive TV a disappointment. The games are inferior and the "whole world to explore" is just a bunch of big companies selling stuff. There will be little of the internet's democratic, even anarchic variety. But TV viewers will like it, and the internet itself will become more bland and corporate as a result.

Meanwhile, a series of long term changes will take place in how we live. Like the fictional family "the Viewers", we will re-arrange our homes to make room for interactive TV. Furniture will shift and appointments will be made and broken. You may watch fewer shows. But you will spend more time using branded services, shopping online, or playing games. Expect programmes to beg for your loyalty and offer you prizes for greater involvement.

While losing some of your "veg out" time, television providers hope to capture areas of your active life. Instead of going out for something, you may order it at home. Instead of asking for it on the phone, you will often just click a button. Convenient replacements will be offered for many personal interactions, and you will depend more and more on your "window on the world".

"That's the TV model," says Howard Hughes "And if you thought television was a dominant force in people's lifestyle's, you are going to see an explosion in the future."

If such a model of life is about to increase its influence explosively, you can expect to witness an increase in the effects television has already had on people's lives. Aside from news stories and sitcom plots about the possible benefits, listen out for news of an increase in television's negative effects. – isolation, poor health, depression, loss of communication in families, hyperactivity in children, unrealistic fear of crime, decline in civic participation and so on.

They Sell You A Lifestyle, You Buy A Society

As people become accustomed to interactive TV, they will begin to question its effect on their homes. Praise for the new technology will give way to questions, such as "Is this just television after all?" and "What is all this about the television gathering information about me?"

When suspicion grows that the goodies offered straight out of the interactive box come with strings, a crucial point will have been reached. The positioning will be over, the public debate will have begun and it will be time for the technology's promoters to defend the benefits of the interactive TV lifestyle.

"They'll say 'How did I live without this?'" says Virginia McMullan of NTL, using an argument you can expect to hear often, "They'll have this wealth of information and entertainment. It's a convenience really, in a time-poor society."

She is right that interactive TV will provide information and entertainment, although it will be tightly controlled, and ever-so-slightly biased, just like TV is today. But she has little to offer the "time poor society". This phrase is becoming increasingly common with social commentators, and is set to become a political issue. It describes the result of people working too hard, recreating too hard, trying to cram too much into their lives, with so little support from others, that men, women and children are all suffering from stress and depression.

McMullan offers TV as a solution. She thinks we will save minutes here and there by looking up train times and buying lawn mowers through our set top boxes. But her job is to encourage viewers to do more with their TV sets, so she ignores the hours of precious leisure time people could gain by watching less television. She ignores television's own contribution to stress. (People who get rid of their TVs entirely find they have doubled their free time. In fact, they write letters to White Dot saying "How did I live without this?")

Exhaustion is not the only social problem that television providers will claim to solve. In his paper 'Key Marketing Issues in Attracting Interactive Users', Andrew Curry used much of the language we can expect to hear when interactive TV fights its corner in our living rooms. He has now left cable television and does research at the Henley Centre for Forecasting, a respected think tank. But while still making interactive TV, he advised his fellow broadcasters to spend more time asking how their product would fit into people's lives.

"What are we marketing?" he writes, "I believe that we are marketing a desire for connection, for control, for engagement."

And he goes on to describe our equivalent of Turner's 'Rain

Steam and Speed', what he thinks will come to represent our excitement about the life interactive technology offers at the end of the 20th century:

"The great painting or photograph, or even bitmapped image, of the cyberspace age has yet to be produced. When it is, it will be about our desire for re-connection. For that is what interactive media can do for us."

Curry is right about our desire for connection. Anyone who has watched *Friends* or the Australian soap opera *Neighbours*, or *Cheers — the place where everybody knows your name* can see how programmers exploit our desire to be with other people again. But is television the cure? The evidence is pretty good that television cut away our connections in the first place. It ate up the time and replaced the need for human contact that led people to combine in groups.

In his essay, Curry emphasised the importance of process over content — that what will keep people watching interactive TV, as opposed to ordinary TV, is not celebrities or Hollywood characters, but a stimulating "human-computer experience". And he is right that the act of watching a box and clicking buttons is more important than what a viewer sees. But what process does he ignore? The process that interactive television has been designed to run, from the start, is one of control. Curry does not mention the computer-human experience that excites television providers — observing people, recording what they do and adapting content to then change their behaviour.

Instead, following Curry's advice, the promoters of interactive television will announce, with fanfare, that they have sold back to us all the life that we've been missing while we were watching so much television. A new machine, they'll say, is bringing people and relaxation back into our lonely, overworked lives.

Expect to see articles about families who play video games together, friendships that start in chat rooms devoted to situation comedies, marriages performed through television sets and the astounding phenomenon of viewers clicking their way to democratic empowerment after some celebrity's interactive TV appeal. Then look out for the first story of a TV set saving someone's life: perhaps a grandmother lying on the floor of her kitchen, unable to get up, whose television notices that she has missed her favourite soap opera that day and phones a neighbour.

"Thank God for my TV," you can imagine her saying, "It's almost like having a friend."

Will any of this repair the damage TV has done? Will it restore our attention spans or give us back the time to ourselves, the long conversations or the communal activity that people of previous generations took for granted? Of course not. But most viewers weren't alive to remember that anyway. They will enthusiastically welcome the new "tertiary relationships" that interactive television provides. They will be keen to add their isolated comments to those of hundreds of other people who read their favourite magazine or drink their favourite beer, and happened to be watching TV at that same hour.

With luck, interactive's promoters will succeed in protecting this re-glamourised television. It will be kept at the centre of our "intelligent homes" and "thinking living spaces" where refrigerators know our name and we no longer have to push the buttons on our automatic garage doors, before driving straight in and hearing them close, reassuringly, behind us. We will buy the interactive TV lifestyle, and leave it free to introduce or hasten changes in our society.

A police officer in charge of mounting closed circuit television (CCTV) cameras on 30 foot, spiked poles, all over towns in the southeast of England once explained his work by quoting Ben Franklin. "The price of liberty," he said, with a straight face, "is eternal vigilance." I still don't know if he was joking. But most books and articles about civil liberties contain this message. The common approach draws attention to a small loss of freedom or abuse of official power. Then the author explains how, in some future time, the infringement will give birth to obvious crimes, and it may be too late.

That is not the approach taken in this book, because interactive television is not something tiny or subtle that could lead to something big. Interactive television is the something big. And it is not just civil libertarians who invent in our nervous imaginations what these companies might do. It is the people themselves who work at these companies who talk excitedly about their new power.

"I can tell you loads of things about Brighton," says Neal Muranyi of the Database Group, "I can tell you wonderful things about the electoral roll, lifestyle data, demographic data. I can get huge amounts of information off that, okay? If only I could then start to segment those households further by their behaviours or their emotions or their personal likes and dislikes from their TV viewing, it's fantastic. It's phenomenal!"

Interactive television is not some first step towards the loss of a freedom, but its wholesale destruction. When you have put a computer into every single home to monitor what people do there, what is left to infringe? As Sun chief executive Scott McNealy has been quoted as saying, "You already have zero privacy – get over it."

Civil liberties are always being redrawn. But, until now, a family's front door was where everything stopped. With the exception of suspects in serious criminal cases, under investigation by law enforcement officers, who have obtained signed warrants from a judge, no one expects to be observed in their own home, much less experimented on.

In 1997 Stephen Graham, a lecturer in town planning at Newcastle University, told a conference on closed circuit television (CCTV) that cameras were covering the entire population of Britain in the same way that water, gas, electricity and then telephony had done this century, and that surveillance would soon be "a fifth utility". Even he did not consider that such a utility would be plumbed into people's houses. But his concluding statement, on how surveillance would change public life, applies equally to the way that interactive TV will soon change how we live in private. "We'll see it as invisible," he said, "we'll expect it to be there".

In order for interactive television to exist as a medium, viewers must be made accustomed to life under its observation. As they play along with games on screen, they will get used to the idea that their TV sets gather information, and use it to play on their emotions. People may eventually welcome this, and feel that the burden of their search for meaning in life is shared with an intelligent friend. Or they may think themselves hip enough to see through the TV set's attempts to manipulate them. Either way, they will keep playing, and their televisions will keep manipulating.

If someday the critics of interactive television are reassured by guarantees that all viewer data is safely locked away, and cannot be abused, then they will have missed their chance to demand that no such information be gathered in the first place. When pundits someday argue about how artificial intelligence should be used to shape individual behaviour, it will mean they no longer consider it newsworthy to question that a machine should exercise such control over human beings.

And if today viewers buy the argument that their interactive televisions are not spying on them, but only customising themselves to viewer desires, then they will have made an important adjustment in their own minds. They will have accepted observation in their own living rooms, every day, by anonymous groups whom they nonetheless understand to be wealthy and powerful. Viewers will have accepted that business and government, the powers that be, have a right to do this.

Such a mental adjustment is new to the countries now developing interactive television. The saying "an Englishman's home is his castle" describes a concept of privacy that goes back to the Magna Carta. The American revolution was fought, in part, against the unreasonable search or use of people's homes. In the two world wars, privacy was one of the democratic liberties that most soldiers thought they were defending. During the entire cold war, it was phone taping and secret observation that embodied what was wrong with communism.

And if citizens of western democracies surrender this principle of individual privacy to a home entertainment appliance, more than just a lifestyle will change.

Like excitement about the promise of technology, fear of technology goes in and out of fashion. A few decades ago, it might have made a great impression upon readers to say that interactive TV "sounds like Big Brother". But by now the term Orwellian is a painful cliché and most people assume that his vision of the future will either never happen, or has already happened, and it was okay after all. As with Vance Packard, you just can't worry about everything all the time. Orwell is no longer cool.

So we include the following quotation from *1984*, not because we expect instant credibility with readers, but in spite of the credibility we will lose by mentioning a prophecy that failed 15 years ago. The thing is, we don't have a choice. His insights seem like common knowledge, and few other writers have bothered to imagine a world without privacy since his book was published, precisely because Orwell did such a good job. He thought this issue all the way through. And the most tangible, memorable element of his novel was a machine:

> "The telescreen received and transmitted simultaneously... There was of course no way of knowing whether you were being watched at any given moment. How often, or on what system the Thought Police plugged in on any individual wire was guesswork. It was even conceivable that they watched everybody all the time. But at any rate they could plug in your wire whenever they wanted to. You had to live – did live, from habit that became instinct – in the assumption that every sound you made was overheard, and, except in darkness, every movement scrutinised."

That machine has now been invented. It is on sale. The camera and the microphone are just tomorrow's peripherals. We have our watchers. We expect them to be there. We will have to get over it.

And is it paranoid to say "I think the government is gathering information and sending me messages through my TV set"? Not if you live in a country where soap operas encourage sterilisation, or if you live in Britain, where the government has been in meetings with television producers about creating something called "Citizen TV".

Steve Morrison, the chief executive of the Granada Media Group wrote in *The Guardian* that the idea for channels offering individualised health advice, education and government services was "born" in his head two years ago. But, of course, various think tanks, consultants and government departments had been kicking similar projects around for years.

Morrison plans to capitalise on digital TV's "ability to build up a profile of individual users to deliver a personalised stream of programming and data". He says such TV could also engage citizens in town hall debates or other multi-way discussions, and so end the "so-called crisis of participation". He imagines viewers tuning in to renew their car tax, but then staying to argue how that money should be spent, "exercising your rights and fulfiling your responsibilities all in one place".

And as "Citizen TV may sound Orwellian to some", he recommends that services from other organisations be offered along side the government ones, and that the service itself be run by an independent media organisation.

Morrison's vision of government bringing services closer to the citizen is laudable, but his vision of democratic participation through "town hall meetings" and other focus groups is unconvincing. His concept of a TV set, linked to the government, transmitting and receiving from people's homes to build up viewer profiles, which is still somehow not Orwellian – requires a leap of faith.

Could interactive television be used as a tool of political power, or even oppression?

It is interesting to note how often, when marketers are asked to describe how interactive TV will alter its messages for different consumers, the first thing that comes to their minds is environmentalists. Here Jonathan Plowden Roberts describes how a car advertisement might be customised for a viewer:

"If you're picking up lots of information from the types of programmes they're watching, you might be able to identify 'well, this person watches all of the programmes to do with social issues'. Well, then don't tell them how wonderfully thirsty this car is. You might talk to them about the fact that everything on this car is recyclable."

With interactive television, everybody hears whatever makes them feel good. Members of any effective consumer movement like environmentalism can be nicely misled with individualised messages.

From there, it is a short step over to politics, where this kind of dissembling has a long history. Politicians, as one marketer called them, are "the kings of relationship marketing" and a television capable of observing everyone and telling each household something different is their perfect medium. Political parties and pressure groups have long known the value of being able to target a single neighbourhood or a particular type of voter. Expect to see people who dress and talk exactly like you sitting around their kitchen tables saying "I just don't trust the government's new plan to regulate cod fisheries…"

Let us take a brief look at how politicians and political groups already use their town hall meetings, personal profiles and the latest technology. To begin, we ask: Could what you watch on TV begin to affect what happens away from the TV? Or, to put it another way:

What could sound more paranoid than someone saying: "I think people I meet are speaking from a script. The scripts are written by the same people who have been sending me messages through the TV set"?

But that is exactly the kind of cross-platform approach that marketers are now putting into place. Phil Swain of Cable and Wireless, for instance, points out that what you watch on TV will soon inform the selection of banner advertisements you are shown on the internet, and vice versa. The next generation of electronic gadgets will allow those customised messages to be placed everywhere.

And, since human beings are just another way of interacting with customers, your viewing behaviour will also inform their choice of conversation with you. Right now, if you call Capital One, a credit card provider, artificial intelligence looks over your past dealings and makes a guess about why you are calling. It flashes advice to the call centre operator, even before he or she picks up the phone to answer. Telephone call centres regularly use your history of past business, and databases of staff comments, to make conversations with paid operators feel like friendly chats. Operators work from a script, chosen according to the type of information their computer holds about you.

"Mrs. Foster, nice to hear from you again. How are your cats, Binky and Coco?"

This technique encourages callers to think of operators as friends, so they keep their business there or buy more stuff. In the future, television will offer anyone this infrastructure to imitate human relationships. It might not get the names of your cats, but your television provider's database will be able to flash advice to an operator's screen such as:

• Loves animals
• Lives alone
• High companionship needs
• Cartoons on regular weekends – grandchildren?
• High interest in current affairs, politics
• Middle to left wing views

Now go on, pretend you are the operator at a catalogue company that uses this technique. Try to get Mrs. Foster to buy something.

Easy, isn't it? And in real life you will have help from artificial intelligence using such logic as:

- If customer is over 60 then say…
- If customer is politically left wing then say…
- If customer lives alone then say…

One to one marketing demands that all a consumer's interactions with a brand be linked into a single relationship. As different marketing, advertising, sales, delivery and customer service applications come to share the same back-end databases, and are in turn used by marketers, salesmen, front office staff and customer service representatives, much of what happens in your real life, away from the television, will become tied to the consumer profile that your television helped to create.

Taken to its logical conclusion, expect that much of your real life will be customised, or simulated. Carol Herman of Grey Advertising told the author of a book about children and consumerism "It isn't enough just to advertise on television… You've got to reach kids throughout their day – in school, as they're shopping at the mall… or at the movies. You've got to become part of the fabric of their lives," Even that statement assumes a natural fabric of life where children live. What if, instead of becoming part of an existing fabric, advertisers are able to replace it, or form it in the first place?

Like *1984*, Peter Weir's 1997 movie *The Truman Show* is already discussed more as a concept than a work of art. Unbeknownst to the lead character, Truman, he has lived his whole life inside a television show. Truman's entire visible world is a sound stage. All his friends, family and acquaintances are actors. and as one of them tells the camera, out of his hearing, "Nothing is fake. It's just… controlled." The action of the film takes place in the week that Turman realises his situation and tries to escape.

While this film can be seen to parody the life of people in television, it is an even better metaphor for the lives of viewers. TV has always sought to keep its audience living in a small, artificial world, no more than ten feet from their sets. We have all been encouraged to spend evenings, weekends and family holidays with simulated friends and their vicarious thrills. As with Truman, the longer we were kept there, the more money somebody makes.

Now the viewer is threatening to escape. But unlike the producer of *The Truman Show*, who can only watch as his hero walks out through a door in the plasterboard sky, television providers are in a position to follow us. So the people you meet, services you use, speeches and actions of your local politicians, and any media you see anywhere, can all be made to do whatever has been found to modify or reinforce your existing behaviour.

Sheldon Rampton is co-author, with John Stauber, of the 1995 book *Toxic Sludge Is Good For You: Lies, Damn Lies and the Public Relations Industry*. It documents the size and power of an industry most of us know nothing about. We all talk about "spin" and "publicity stunts", but such phrases suggest amateurish efforts to snatch tiny bits of attention. We think we can see through our politicians and any techniques that companies use to get their names in the papers.

The work of Stauber and Rampton, however, makes clear how misfounded that confidence is:

- Between them the top PR firms in America earned $1.04 billion in 1995.
- About 40% of all news is planted directly , almost unedited, by public relations firms
- PR firms act as private intelligence agencies, gathering information on journalists, citizens or activist groups and anyone else who might be critical of their clients.
- The industry has run government propaganda efforts in many countries. The more democratic a country, the better funded and more sophisticated is the work of these companies to control it.
- Civilian nuclear energy and the Nicaraguan contra army were both invented by public relations firms. They are just two examples of the ambitious scale and long term planning that PR firms can bring to the control of public life.

Their book documents the truth of something they quote from another author, Alex Carey:

"The twentieth century has been characterised by three developments of great political importance: the growth of democracy, the growth of corporate power, and the growth of corporate propaganda as a means of protecting corporate power against democracy."

It makes for grim reading. After all, what could be more paranoid than saying this:

"The conscious and intelligent manipulation of the organised habits and opinions of the masses is an important element in democratic society. Those who manipulate this unseen mechanism of society constitute an invisible government which is the true ruling power of our country"

But that quote isn't from *Toxic Sludge*. They are the first words of the book *Propaganda*, by Edward Bernays, the father of public relations. He saw it as his job to shape people's view of the world. But his aim was never any such airy-fairy concept as "creating culture". It was the increased power and wealth of certain groups of people – their projects, their companies, their political parties. As Bernays told a biographer late in his life: "We didn't deal in image, we dealt in reality".

And a quick look at how PR firms go about their business is enough to see how important interactive TV will become to them:

- A firm called Qest (sic) offers software which acts as a radar, allowing companies to plot interest groups on a graph by their strength and likely opposition.
- A firm called Marketing Research Institute sell their clients something called "DNA" – Demographic Niche Attributes – for "grass roots targeting". They help corporations and right wing causes target individuals with customised material.
- A firm called National Grassroots and Communications specialises in breaking down local opposition to any of their client's projects.
- A firm called Optima Direct specialises in creating false grassroots democracy (astroturf). Within hours of an issue arising to cause trouble for a client, such as Phillip Morris or the National Rifle Association, they can have their call centres manned by hundreds of staff, calling everyone in an area. Vice president Mike Malik told Stauber and Rampton how he uses telephones to refine a message: "…you're on the phones today, you analyse the results, you change your script and try a new thing tomorrow. In a three-day program you can make four or five different changes,

find out what's really working, what messages really motivate people, and improve your response rates."

- Where public relations and technology are doing the most to change the face of American democracy is in the headquarters of Ralph Reed's Christian Coalition in Virginia, capable of generating 100,000 calls in a weekend. Reed told a conference of PR executives how the Coalition managed to derail the political career of a Virginia politician whom it did not care for. After surveying everyone in key constituencies, they were able to find what issue every household cared about most. For some people, the main issue was water. For others, it was crime. On election day, Reed had only to send out pamphlets telling one house that his preferred candidate was "the water candidate" and another that his man was "the crime candidate" and so on. His candidate won a seat that had been held by the Democrats since the Civil War. Reed told his audience: "There is no replacement for knowing what somebody cares about."

Public relations firms use the methods and technology of direct marketing, not just to "get a message out", but to control opinion, confuse issues, break down opposition groups and gain territory. If this sounds military, that's because it is. Stauber and Rampton document numerous contacts, and a real cultural bond, between the American public relations industry, the CIA and the Pentagon. They list the activities of Raphel Pagan and Jack Mongoven, who specialise in "public policy intelligence" – snooping on environmentalist and consumer groups.

Raphel came to public relations out of the military and Jack is fond of quoting Carl Von Clausewitz's *Nine Principles of War* and Sun Tzu's *The Art of War*. This knowledge of martial strategy served them well in 1989, when they worked for the Nestlé corporation. By investigating and profiling each group that backed an international boycott of Nestlé's products, and then targeting each group individually, the pair were able to dismantle their opposition's support.

Jack Mongoven's son, Bart works with his father. And Sheldon Rampton tells the story of an environmental group in Australia who got a questionnaire from Bart, asking all about their activities. The cover letter explained that the survey would help enhance understanding and communications between business groups and environmentalists. But the person opening the letter had read Stauber and Rampton's book and sent the questionnaire to them instead.

"It's an example," says Rampton, "of how tireless they are about collecting information. And how there's this huge gap between what they say they want the information for and what they really want it for. They're collecting information on environmental groups, and shmoozing them up by saying 'we just want to improve communication' while to their clients, internally, they're saying 'This is war!' and 'We have to mobilise against these people'".

Asking questions, explaining that it will help serve people better, then using the information against them... does any of that sound familiar? If this is war, then interactive television is the equivalent of handing public relations firms like Mongoven's the atom bomb.

- It will give them the profiles they need of neighbourhoods, organisations and the psychological make up of individuals who belong to them.
- It will give them the ability to offer discrete messages to different people, telling everybody whatever they want to hear about their clients
- It will allow them to monitor support and involvement with issues

The pressure that editors and producers come under to please their advertisers, especially in the United States, will certainly grow as it becomes possible to aim programming variations at individual television sets. When your own personalised newspaper says "Here are some news items I thought would interest you!" How can you be sure it wasn't someone else's idea? Journalistic integrity will be impossible to determine or even discuss if everyone is offered something different.

In fact, all of public life now depends on the idea of a single reputation in public. When a company or a government does anything in the open, everyone in the country sees that same company or government do the same thing and can hold them responsible. In the future, that may not be true. Any organisation will be able to make as many different public announcements as there are interactive television sets. Saying different things to different people used to be called duplicity. Now it has been rebranded as customisation. Soon it will be the norm.

To run through an example of these techniques working together on interactive television, pretend your local utility has decided to build a nuclear waste dump in your back yard. You don't like this, and decide to do something about it. So you print up some leaflets and walk out of your house to meet your neighbours and ask for their support. This is the advantage that the little guy has traditionally had when standing up to the marketing, legal and mass media power of industry or government – grass roots organising within the intimacy of the doorstep.

In the past, you might have known the people on your block from your involvement in community activities. Now you have to introduce yourself. But before you've knocked on your first door, the utility or their public relations firm has been able to use interactive television to do the following:

- Identify you as a likely opponent
- Predict the arguments you will make
- Predict the houses you will knock on
- Predict your likely allies, opponents or anyone who might be persuaded to disrupt your campaign
- Show different ads to each group, perhaps parodying the efforts of someone just like you
- Profile the motivations of everyone in your neighbourhood
- Create an astroturf group, perhaps called "Jobs for Yourtown" and know who is most likely to join

Because direct marketing is, by its nature, discreet, you do not know any of this has been happening. You believe yourself to be taking part in a democratic process, while the real action is happening outside it, in a computer somewhere.

Another interesting cultural bond is the one between the military intelligence community and one to one marketing. For example, before joining Synergy, Pat Dade worked on ECHELON, a computer system developed by the US military and the National Security Agency (NSA), capable of monitoring every fax, email and telephone conversation in the world. "Oh yeah," Dade laughs, "We spied on everything."

Dade is not the only intelligence expert to have found a natural home in the marketing departments of tomorrow. Adaptive systems and neural networks of all kinds were first developed to spy on people, and many of the companies that developed this software now specialise in one to one. Outside the laws which apply to other citizens, these professionals have spent careers using software that monitors people's private lives. That experience will have shaped their attitudes. And now they have made it their business to shape yours.

So, a question: In the case of the waste disposal plant, what is the difference between your campaign against the plant and the campaign for jobs, organised by the utility using a call centre and interactive advertising?

The differences are surprisingly hard to pin down. Both sides would use rhetoric, both would tend to tell their own story and ignore the other side, both would print leaflets and use whatever media they could afford, both would have a strategy, both would be protecting their interests, their public image, both would use logos or headed stationery to make themselves memorable to the public, both would try to tailor their message to reach whatever audience they were addressing.

Some people would say there is no difference between them. Edward Bernays wrote many times that he was a democrat and a patriot. For people like Bernays, all is fair in love, war and politics. Everyone is out for themselves, everyone is advertising and propaganda is just another form of free speech.

All of which is true of course, and presents no problem, as long as you don't care who holds power in your democracy. But this system, which guarantees free speech, was established by people who held strong views about power. And if you think democracy should put power into the hands of the many instead of the few, then there is a very big difference between the two campaigns: one of them is fake. It pretends to come from ordinary citizens who live in the area, where in reality it has been created elsewhere precisely to manipulate them.

What is the difference?

- Between a real campaign and a public relations astroturf campaign?
- Between a petition and a marketing survey?
- Between a political meeting and a focus group?

The answer is always the same: It is the difference between committing yourself to an outcome and just giving up opinions, or the difference between speaking out and having someone eavesdrop. You could say one is action, and the other is just behaviour. Either people take responsibility and do things for themselves, or they are invited to take part in something run by somebody else, for somebody else's reasons.

The demagogue, the propagandist and the plutocrat are natural members of any democracy, always seeking ways to use it for their own wealth and power. Ordinary citizens have always known it was their job to keep them in check. Starting now, that may no longer be possible.

We spell this out not to damn public relations firms, big business, government bureaucrats or wealthy individuals, but to warn that interactive television has been designed, from the beginning, as their tool. Sitting in every living room, this new technology will have solved all their problems and overcome all the limits that were placed in their way.

Pat Dade doesn't see any problem with interactive TV. Given the example of a woman protesting the construction of a nuclear waste dump in her back yard, he doesn't think she will be disadvantaged.

"She'll have her own web page," says Dade, and predicts that the strength of her argument will always outweigh slick advertising from her utility, no matter how well targeted. But if that is the case, then what does his company do for a living? Don't Synergy's profiles provide something for companies that rational argument on its own cannot?

"Yes, in a way. Yes," he admits, but later responds: "We work for people who don't pay us. We work for universities, we work for students to help them understand what's going on."

So his answer, in other words, is that a good cause will raise enough money or sympathy to get the services of his firm. If the woman fighting the utility is really lucky, the Watchers will start helping her. Dade believes interactive television will be just another tool of democratic free speech. But if Dade is right, and this is how things work in the future, then real democracy, where people do know each other's names and do real grass roots organisation, will be programmed out of existence. And what takes its place may not be fake, just… controlled.

That portrait of the cyber-age that Andrew Curry wants to see, the one illustrating how we live when our need for re-connection is finally met by our televisions, maybe it's the Truman Show. As time goes on, anyone who does business, informs or entertains you will, by coincidence, be like you. They will look like you, talk like you, have your interests and share your views. Following on from your interactive television, an entire world of public interactions will be scripted.

Sheldon Rampton gives a small example of how such artificial worlds are already created by companies protecting their image. A food critic for a newspaper told Rampton how he had walked into a restaurant, without announcing himself, and asked to see a menu. It just so happened the night's special was glazed livers, his favourite dish. The critic enjoyed the meal, went home and gave the restaurant a great review. But his girlfriend, who worked for a public relations firm, was less impressed. "You sap," she said "They knew you were coming. They knew all about you."

This scene would make a nice subplot in a situation comedy. But it becomes less funny if, as Rampton says, such deception is part of an increasing trend. Rampton can name a number of agencies that specialise in collecting information about journalists – their politics, their hobbies, what clubs they join, even their favourite dish.

"When you think about that level of massaging reality," says Rampton, "so you anticipate where the person is coming from and create a temporary reality, tailored to that person – that's what they're doing now, without digital TV. But what you're talking about is introducing that into the home, where it becomes like your permanent babysitter, monitoring you constantly as an individual."

The emerging combination of psychographics, one to one marketing and interactive television creates a new model of citizenship. You sit on a couch and the TV gathers information about you. A main computer behind the TV relays that information to companies and governments, who then respond with products, policies, legal administration and more television.

Now, is that a perfect model of democracy, whereby powerful institutions respond to your every wish? Or, is it the perfect subversion of democracy, whereby your every move is studied and every fear or desire manipulated, thereby handing huge control to the people who pay for what is shown?

It need not have been like this. The technology exists to create services that do not observe or manipulate consumers. Interactivity, e-commerce, and even elements of one to one marketing could all be deployed in ways that gave real power to individuals. But nobody is doing that here. It wouldn't be television.

They Sell You A Society, You End Up Buying An Identity

At some point, the interactive TV lifestyle will come under real criticism. Commentators, religious leaders and artists will begin to miss privacy. They will cast around for ways to describe some feeling or way of life that is missing. The relationship between people everywhere will have changed. The relationship between people and power will have become hopelessly complicated, difficult to understand.

At that point, the public relations plan for interactive TV will have to spread a new, post-post-modern attitude. Available in five colours, warm to the touch and smelling of sex, a new, caring ethos of community will be evoked when interactive TV's defenders say "Like it or not, interactive TV is now part of our culture, part of who we are." And when you hear that, you'll know the game is over. They'll have achieved everything they set out to achieve.

Psychologists talk about "selving". It's a verb — the act of defining your self as part of, and separate from, the world. How are people going to define themselves in the future, when all their actions are monitored and fed into a system that colours everything around them? How will you put together a sane version of yourself, when a paranoid schizophrenic's delusion with your name on it is being built around you? When the boundary between what is you and what is not you has been deliberately dismantled, what can you grab hold of?

Brands of course. "Everyone's the same except for their branding," says Pat Dade, "Everyone will be their own brand." This is a commonly stated idea. Walk into your media studies course and say this; everyone will click their fingers. Like many who study media, Dade envisions a world of people who make ready use of their creativity and intellectual curiosity. The merit of what he does depends on citizens who are politically active and socially engaged, and need only the tools with which to complete their own life's work. Grabbing images and ideas from the media and reworking them into their own image, these players in the great post-modern game enjoy the freedom to create their own identities from scratch.

But that's not how things really work, is it?

Interactive TV, for instance, doesn't provide some kind of psychic workspace where viewers fashion themselves. That would leave too much to chance. Like television before it, interactive TV is designed to guide and influence its viewers. Manufacturers don't just provide the bits and pieces which a dynamic new generation uses for its own ends, they make it their business to make those bits and pieces the ends in themselves.

Anyone seeking to fashion their own identity from scratch is better off getting away from manufacturers for a while. One to one marketing on interactive media has been designed to coax as many of us as close to them as possible. And, in exchange for a little convenience, most of us will play along. We don't need to bother creating our own brands because we happily patch ourselves together out of the ones available for free. Where would you go to find curious, creative, active, engaged citizens? Never in front of a TV set.

If you are on the internet, visit www.thepalace.com. It is a system of customised chat rooms and virtual spaces where you can scan in a picture and then represent yourself as whoever you want to be. When other people stand in the The Palace, they will see your words come out of a speech bubble from whoever you say you are. You could be anything – a snake, a fish, a monster. People can even trade identities in the middle of conversations. Surely, this is an early example of the future where everyone is their own brand.

But notice how many rooms in The Palace are named "Star Wars" and "Pokemon". "It's depressing," says one visitor, "Everybody is Bart Simpson or Kenny from *South Park*."

Given a choice to be anyone or anything in the world, these people choose to be characters from TV shows and singers in rock bands. Given a chance to say anything in the world, these people seize a chance to say the things those characters would say. Bart®, Homer®, Kenny® and the whole gang are commercial brands, and you can't get any more involved with a brand than choosing to become it. This is how things will work for most people who watch interactive TV.

Group identification is part of life. But in the past, it obviously resulted from close contact with other human beings. Any group identification beyond that was either very important and required conviction, (religion, country, class, loyalty to some cause like a trade union movement) or it had little influence on an individual's life and required no conviction (people who drank the same beer).

These days, we have little group identification with other humans. And group identification beyond that is easier and more relaxed. Great causes can spring from nowhere and disappear again. And it is now possible to identify with a very important cause or group of people without even knowing of its existence. Likewise, it is possible to hold with great conviction the opinions and attitudes of a group that doesn't even exist, and is nothing more than a brand. In fact, it is now possible to make up such group identities willy-nilly and use them as hoops for people to jump through.

This is what Pat Dade does for a living. At the top of Maslow's hierarchy of needs, your desire for self-actualisation can only be filled by something which then becomes you. Anyone selling into that desire makes you one of them. Selving, like anything else, is now offered as a service, and interactive TV won't just sell you products. It will nurture you, raising you up, over years, into one of the numerous selves that sponsors have made available for actualisation. Your TV is the two way link between you and some new form of communal, commercial, disposable identity.

When you meet any post-modern hipster, covered in logos and talking in lines from shaving commercials and sitcom reruns, who is it that stands before you? What kind of selving has been going on? And he is just a crude prototype of the people you will meet when interactive TV is "part of who we are".

The truth is, we will be part of it.

Today interactive TV is being marketed as a box of tricks and goodies. Like any machine, it is a reliable system of inputs and outputs. You click on the handset or type something into your keyboard and get what you want from the machine.

But what if you, sitting in front of your TV also form a reliable system of inputs and outputs? Then you are also a machine. This is the real application of interactive television. Somebody with a keyboard somewhere types in what he wants and his machine, including you and your TV set, output the behaviour that he requested.

Who is that person? You'll never know. But anyone who works in computers can tell you how much fun he will be having. Some of the people who have helped with this book work in computers, and we've sat in the bar, just thinking up all the things we could do to people if we had a software application monitoring them in their living rooms, how we could hook up and start manipulating all the bits of their lives. And we're supposed to be civil libertarians! But we're also professionals, and programming is what we do for a living. It is only natural for professionals like us to integrate people like you into the systems and machines we control. As professionals, we won't rest until a system works just right, until it gives us anything we choose at the touch of a button, until we are empowered.

Only one thing stops programmers of any kind from treating your free will as a technical problem to be overcome, and that is privacy. It's the break in the circuit that means your life will never function properly as part of someone else's video game. With it, you are beyond the reach of any company, political party or government who seeks to play your God, no matter how powerful they are, or sophisticated their methods. Without it, you will be vulnerable to every fabric softener bully and smiling, animated child seducer.

It is tempting to conclude this chapter with a grave warning. But, as any behavioural marketer knows, that might put readers off. So here is a quote from the radical, but undelivered, first draft of George Washington's Inaugural Speech, 30th of April, 1789. This missing page of the speech was only discovered in 1996, beneath a sofa in the English village of Aldeburgh. Washington has just finished describing a future time when America falls apart, and notice how the President tempers his strong fear-inducing message with a happy ending:

> "...but until the people of America shall have lost all virtue; until they shall have become totally insensible to the difference between freedom and slavery; until they shall have been reduced to such poverty of spirit as to be willing to sell that pre-eminent blessing, the birthright of Freeman, for a mess of pottage; in short, until they shall have been found incapable of governing themselves and ripe for a Master — those consequences, I think, can never arrive."

So lighten up! There's nothing to worry about.

Free

REALLY, THERE'S NOTHING TO WORRY ABOUT. Digital interactive television is going to fail. Technophiles know a second-rate product when they see one and complaints are already beginning to surface about the "walled garden" in which viewers are confined. And if the industry thinks they can hide their viewer observation and viewer manipulation until everyone is used to it, they're mistaken. People who care about privacy are not going to let that happen.

Sure, nobody likes to miss out. Liz Camps of Digital TV Report is right to advise her industry to "create a mystique of empowerment around the DTV device". She understands that talk of a "digital revolution" will encourage people to think that cool, interesting people are all taking control of their lives by using powerful new devices. The all important early adopters, who make or break the fortunes of consumer technology, are always listening out for such talk. And, as Camps also points out, the "enlightenment seekers" are out there, waiting for the next big wave of social change to include and empower them.

But they will be disappointed. In fact, rather than salivate together over the launch of interactive TV, the next big consumer trend will see early adopters and enlightenment seekers celebrating their part in its death. Jim Nail of the internet research firm Forrester Research was asked by the New York Times about advertisers who link on and off-line data. He described a kind of user empowerment very different from the one Liz Camps was advocating:

"Privacy is potentially a huge sleeper issue," he said. "You see a lot of talk and some government action on it, but it hasn't really caught fire with the public yet. This has the potential to touch it off."

Just as intrusive marketing methods gain their most powerful technological weapons, they will meet their first organised resistance. The issue of privacy on the internet already incites passionate debate across a range of other issues. Privacy in front of the television set is even more important.

Viewer, Escape!

Talk of a "digital revolution" is unhelpful. It encourages people to think of any new technology as inevitable, which is not true. Interactive TV and Video On Demand have both been tried in the marketplace before, and failed. Before this incarnation is anything else, it is just another product that someone is trying to sell you.

Instead of buying, we invite you to become an Early Rejector. Join our boycott of interactive TV and help us tell others the truth about what it is designed to do. Help us create an informed debate about this technology while people are still weighing up the alternatives.

- If you have interactive television, get rid of it. Write a letter to your provider explaining why.
- Write to other interactive TV providers in your area, explaining that you are will not sign up unless they agree to the Demands of Viewer Privacy, listed overleaf.
- Talk to people in the communications chain with television providers. For example, visit a department store that sells digital televisions and say you want one that does not offer interactivity, because you have heard they are designed to monitor and manipulate viewers. Make sure to speak with the manager responsible for buying decisions.
- Write to companies that advertise or offer services on interactive television. Express your disappointment that they have chosen to take part in a business that puts their profit over your civil liberty.
- When writing to companies, it is worthwhile sending two copies: one to the managing director and one to the customer services department.

Self-Regulation Is Not Enough

Interactive television providers seem to be hoping that no one will think to ask questions about privacy. And many people do not because they assume the law already protects them. But they are mistaken.

Britain has no privacy law. So data that is properly collected and stored can be used in any way the television providers can imagine. As Caspar Bowden of the Foundation for Information Policy Research says, "In Europe, Data Protection principles no longer cut it. We don't just need informed consent, we need the right to not be surveilled — whether or not this is part of a freely offered commercial service."

The Demands of Viewer Privacy

- The provider agrees not to gather or sell information about viewers for marketing purposes.
- The provider agrees not to create viewer profiles or to study viewer behaviour with the aim of then influencing viewer attitudes or behaviour.
- The provider agrees not to customise or target any content – advertising, programming or services – with the aim of affecting viewer attitudes or behaviour.
- The provider agrees not to allow interactivity in advertising or branded programming aimed at children.
- The provider agrees to provide viewers with a full explanation of all changes made to any interactive system, and a chance to reject any upgrade at no cost.
- The provider will furnish, through the television if possible, a complete copy of all information the provider holds about the viewer. Where data is unintelligible to anyone but the provider's computer software, it will be converted into easily understood reports.

To make the best of what is available, in the article below Ibrahim Hasan, a solicitor specialising in data protection, gives his view of how Britain's Data Protection Act works with interactive television. Most interesting is his assertion that any viewer should be able to ask for all the personal information held about him or her, and receive it in a form that easily understood. This should force TV providers to hand over explanations of their data, not just a bunch of control codes. But this has not yet been tested, and much of what the Act allows is left to the people enforcing it.

Readers in Britain should look through any interactive television contract and ask themselves whether it gives viewers any adequate warning of how their information will be gathered and used – not just the details written into any contract you sign, but the raw data of your viewing activity. If it doesn't, then it has not met the Act's demand for informed consent.

The United States does not even have a data protection act, and the FCC has recently ruled that no privacy regulation is necessary for the internet. As for interactive TV, a speech to the International Radio and Television Society by FCC Chairman William Kennard called only for faster, more profitable deployment into homes.

"Could this be the convergence we have all been hoping for?" he asked, "I think it is. And it is a great thing – the best marketing minds in TV, electronics, software, entertainment, and other industries are focused on how to develop this new application ... Develop your business plans. Make your investments. And be confident, as I am, that what lies ahead is a bright future."

Maybe he was just working the crowd, but regulation does not seem forthcoming without pressure from somewhere else.

So American readers are faced with a more urgent and difficult task. Before they can demand proper enforcement of privacy legislation, they must convince their Congress to pass some. In the land of the free, consumers at the moment enjoy no protection from firms gathering personal data for marketing purposes.

Television providers everywhere are crossing their fingers, hoping that their dreams of being "data powerhouses" are not limited by future interpretation of the law.

"They have potentially a very lucrative revenue stream there," says Roger Randall of Agency.com about the information broadcasters can collect, "Whether they will be able to access and exploit it properly is down to legislation. And if they can't, they can't. And that will be very crippling in terms of any one to one activity."

It is important to note here that Mr. Randall is not referring to the services viewers want. None of the services that viewers think they are buying require companies like Agency.com to gather information from them. Favourite programmes, screen preferences, video on demand – all these things can be provided without personal data about viewers or their households.

TV shows can even be recommended without a company storing a viewer profile. It is possible, for instance, to save the viewing history on the viewer's box in their home and never send it anywhere, or permit anyone else to see it. Instead, the box itself then makes recommendations from categories of programmes that are broadcast to it. The only information sent out of the home could then be anonymous, used only to update which programmes are put into which categories.

This is the approach taken by a digital television called TiVo, produced by Philips and sold in the United States. TiVo guarantees that no profiling information is ever gathered out of the home, and while such a system could still be used to target advertising, its existence proves that company ownership of viewer data is not necessary to run an interactive system.

No, when Roger Randall worries that legislation could cripple activity, he is referring to the services that television providers plan to offer their corporate and government clients. And it is not in the public interest that these services are left to regulate themselves. They should be crippled, as soon as possible.

At the moment, viewers are not even offered the chance to opt out of such intrusive services. Any cable company is in constant two-way communication with every TV set. And, as mentioned before, British Sky Broadcasting's interactive service, Open, charges viewers hundreds of pounds if they do not allow their set top box to transmit to the company by telephone every night. What used to be a right to privacy is thereby turned into a luxury.

- Write to your representatives in government demanding effective privacy legislation and regulation of interactive TV.
- Write to the broadcasting and data protection regulators in your country, demanding that they put the viewers' right to privacy before the financial gain of the broadcast industry.
- If you believe that a contract you signed did not adequately warn you of the surveillance to which you would be exposed, demand that the regulator help you get compensation.

Contact Us

This boycott is organised by White Dot, the anti-television campaign, and Privacy International, a network of privacy experts and human rights organisations.

White Dot	**White Dot**	**Privacy International**
PO Box 577257	PO Box 2116	Washington Office
Chicago,	Hove, E Sussex	666 Pennsylvania Ave SE
IL 60657	BN3 3LR	Suite 301
USA	United Kingdom	Washington
Attn: Spy TV	Attn: Spy TV	DC 20003 USA
Info@whitedot.org	info@whitedot.org	pi@privacy.org

Although White Dot encourages people to throw their TV sets out the window, we welcome the involvement of people who wish to enjoy TV and privacy at the same time. And it goes without saying

REGULATORS IN BRITAIN

Data Protection Registrar
Wycliffe House
Water Lane
Wilmslow, Cheshire SK9 5AF
01625 545745
www.dataprotection.gov.uk
(This website provides a useful
list of every data protection
office in the world:
http://www.dataprotection.gov.uk/
dpalist.htm)

**Office of Telecommunications
(OFTEL)**
Consumer Representation Section
50 Ludgate Hill
London
EC4M 7JJ
0171 634 8888
http://www.oftel.gov.uk

**Department of Trade
and Industry**
Enquiry Unit
1 Victoria Street
London SW1H 0ET
020 7215 5000
http://www.dti.gov.uk

**Independent Television
Commission**
33 Foley Street
London W1P 7LB
0171 255 3000
http://www.itc.org.uk

REGULATORS IN THE USA

**National Telecommunications
and Information Administration**
Herbert C. Hoover Building
U.S. Department of Commerce /
NTIA
1401 Constitution Ave., N.W.
Washington, D.C. 20230
(202) 482-1840
http://www.ntia.doc.gov

Federal Trade Commission
CRC-240
Washington, D.C. 20580
(877) 382-4357
http://www.ftc.gov

**Federal Communications
Commission**
445 12th St. SW
Washington DC 20554
(202) 418-0190
http://www.fcc.gov/

that any information you send will be used only to return information about this campaign. If you would like to know more about White Dot or Privacy International, please indicate this specifically in your letter.

For the latest news, visit the boycott's web site:
http://www.spytv.co.uk

The following sites also contain information about interactive television:

http://www.whitedot.org	White Dot
http://www.privacy.org	Privacy International
http://www.cme.org	Center for Media Education

Help Sell The Next Big Thing

Without millions of dollars to spend, the promotion of this boycott and any calls for new legislation will require ordinary people to do some promoting on their own. Luckily, as products go, privacy is an easy sell. Civil liberties are the next real "digital revolution" and no savvy consumer wants to miss out on that. Who knows? Orwell might become cool again.

- Tell friends and relatives about interactive TV and this boycott
- Put a line like this one in the signature block of your emails and usenet postings:
  Interactive TV spies on viewers.
  Join the boycott: http://www.spytv.co.uk
- Put copies of our banner ad on your website, using this line:
  <a href="http://www.spytv.co.uk"><img border=0
  src="http://www.spytv.co.uk/images/spybannerad.gif"></a>

Stay On Message

It is worth thinking about this campaign the way marketing and public relations executives do.

- Target early adopters
- Target opinion leaders
- Target enlightenment seekers

Here is a sample pitch:

"Want control? Want to avoid people controlling you? Want empowerment? Want real choice? Want the real world at your fingertips, instead of a fake? Want real interactivity, email and home shopping? Then why pay money to be spied on in your own home? Boycott interactive TV! Who needs it?"

If the customer is argumentative, refer to the following frequently asked questions:

What is wrong with interactive television?

It has been designed from the beginning to gather information about people in their own homes. Using the TV's return path, and artificial intelligence, interactive TV providers do demographic, lifestyle, market segmentation and psychographic analysis of your viewing habits. Such analyses can be combined with externally available data to create an intimate picture of who you are and what motivates you.

Because interactive television is capable of showing something different on every single television, providers plan to use the data they gather to create messages that sell you things or change your thinking. The whole process of trying something, measuring its effect, and trying something else, until your behaviour changes, can be automated. This capability will be sold to companies, governments or just the highest bidder. You will never know exactly who has paid whom to have your computer do what to the way you live. Meanwhile, your computer will, over the years, learn everything it can about you.

This invasion of privacy in the home could be harmful to viewers over time, and will certainly be harmful to democracy.

Isn't interactive TV just like a supermarket loyalty card?

The mechanism is similar, but interactive television is many times more intrusive. The types of analysis that can be done with viewing data are more personal, and the types of manipulation possible are more varied and powerful. Nobody spends four hours a night in their supermarket, nor do they get all their news about the world there. No supermarket loyalty card can record everything you see and hear, nor can the entire shopping environment be changed to influence your individual behaviour.

Isn't interactive TV just like the internet?

The internet and interactive TV share certain functionality. But interactive TV makes some of the privacy problems of the internet worse, while introducing dangerous new ones.

The internet was not designed to identify a person using it, or even that person's computer. There are debates about the ways this might change, and there are methods of identification, such as cookie files, which the user can refuse to accept. But the internet provides more anonymity than interactive television, which not only knows your name, but all the other information you put on any service contract.

The internet is not owned by anyone. If you use a computer, the chances are that the computer belongs to you, and you have control over what the software does. You can install your own software to change how the internet works in your home. With interactive television, the entire network belongs to one company and you have little say over how it chooses to operate the box on your TV set. Software can change without your knowing anything about it.

The internet and TV are used differently. The first is used briefly, for research. The second is used four hours every day by people who are letting their minds unwind. It is a very different environment, one much better for gathering information and manipulating users.

What can anyone really tell about me from my TV viewing?

Television providers themselves are excited about the detailed information they can gather from people over years of viewing. Not only will people answer questions about themselves on the screen, but everything they do can be analysed to create a profile of who they are.

The programmes you watch and the ads you are willing to sit through reveal your interests. Your behaviour in front of the screen, taken as a whole, can be analysed with artificial intelligence to link you to other, similar people. If someone who monitors your viewing knows a great deal about a certain group of similar people, and is then able to say you are one of that group, then they suddenly know a great deal about you. Marketing and database consultancy firms are now gearing up to do just that.

Advertisers, public relations firms and anyone else who pays to use your viewing data can begin to understand where you get your information, how you respond to new events, what motivates you to do things and what kinds of things you want out of life. They will also begin to understand your weaknesses and anxieties. When linked to other, externally available, data, such profiles will allow them to create programming that programs you.

Doesn't the law protect against this kind of thing?

Some countries, such as members of Europe, are protected by data protection laws. Other countries, such as the United States, are not. But even countries that have these laws have not come to grips with this new technology. Many of the decisions about what regulations shall be in force and how they shall be applied are being taken right now. The providers of interactive television hope to make the observation of people in their own homes seem normal and publicly acceptable, while they have the chance.

Why is this a problem if the TV is just selling me things I might want?

Even if that was all the TV did, there would be a problem. Privacy in the home is a 600 year old concept that is fundamental to democracy. With the advent of computers that can monitor and respond to the behaviour of millions of people all at once, such a concept becomes even more important.

But it is already clear that interactive TV will be used for more than just selling. Just as politicians and ideas can be "sold", so interactive TV could allow the entire intellectual life of a country to be monitored and controlled from a single keyboard.

Perhaps most importantly, do you want a machine in your living room that watches you, learns about you and tries to change your behaviour, when you have no control over how it is programmed? When you don't finally know who does? Why? What for? Some email? A little home shopping? You can get that anywhere.

My TV provider has a privacy policy, or belongs to a privacy campaign. Am I protected?

Maybe, maybe not. Such policy statements and industry led campaigns may be designed to make viewers feel secure, while allowing TV providers to continue monitoring. For instance, a promise not to make personal details available to third parties does not stop a company using those details itself on a third party's behalf. Keep in mind that most companies providing interactive TV have been told it is a good investment precisely because of the way viewer data can be used for marketing purposes.

My TV provider says the interactive service could not work without collecting information

Not true. It is perfectly possible to create interactive television that does not collect information about individual households, or collects it in a way that they remain anonymous. And it is certainly possible not to sell the use of that information to third parties.

I don't own a computer, but want to join the "digital revolution"

There is no one digital revolution, but many on offer. Computers are getting cheaper and easier to use all the time and the internet offers a much wider variety of information and services than interactive TV. If you don't like computers, personal organisers and mobile phones are beginning to offer email. As time goes on, there will be many other ways for you to use digital services. Interactive TV, on the other hand, offers a second rate service with some very dangerous strings attached. Why not give it a miss and find something better?

Aren't you just being old fashioned, or scared of technology?

Most of the people who care about this issue work in computers. It is precisely because we are comfortable with technology, and know what it can do, that we are calling this boycott. The Interactive TV now on offer is not new or revolutionary. It is just television providers hoping to refashion the internet as something they control, and can use to manipulate viewers. What could be more old fashioned than that?

Appendix

Interactive Television & Data Protection
By Ibrahim Hasan

IT IS A WELL KNOW FACT the UK has no law of privacy. But there are statutes in place which together give an individual some rights to a private life. Chief amongst these statutes is the Data Protection Act 1984

The act places obligations on those people who record and use information relating to individuals. They must be open about that use and follow sound and proper practices.

It must be understood that the Act does not just apply to information which is held on computer; a common misconception. The Act applies to "personal data". This is defined in section 1(3) of the Act:

"Personal Data means data consisting of information which relates to a living individual who can be identified from the information(or from that and other information in the possession of the data user)..."

Personal data does not have to identify individuals but can be letters, numbers or codes which together with other information held by the data user can identify individuals. Thus it is clear that data collected by interactive TV will be subject to the Act.

Having established this, it is important to know with which provisions the TV companies gathering such information have to comply. Viewers can then begin to fight back by demanding that companies adhere to the Act.

Main Provisions Of The Act

TV companies collecting personal data must: observe the Eight Data Protection Principle, ensure they are registered to process Personal Data and allow Data Subjects to access their Personal Data.

The Eight Principles

Broadly the eight principles governing Personal Data are:
1 Be obtained and processed fairly and lawfully.
2 Be held only for the lawful purposes described in the Data Protection Register.

3 Be used only for those purposes and only be disclosed to those people described in the Register.

4 Be adequate, relevant and not excessive in relation to the purpose for which it is held.

5 Be accurate and where necessary be kept up to date.

6 Be held no longer than is necessary for the registered purpose.

7 Be made available to Data Subjects if requested by them.

8 Be surrounded by proper security.

Generally these are the basis requirements on the companies in relation to their holding of personal data in relation to their subscribers. Whilst breaching these principles is not an automatic criminal offence, apart from principle 3, it can be made a subject of a complaint to the Data Protection Registrar. Thus if for example a viewer realises that a company has information about them which is inaccurate or not up to date then they can complain to the registrar. The Registrar will investigate and then, subject to her findings issue either:

- Search Data Users premises.
- Issue an Enforcement Notice compelling a Data User to take certain steps e.g. destroy any Personal Data.
- Institute criminal proceedings.
- Issue a deregistration notice so hat he company is no longer registered to process data and therefore automatically commits a criminal offence

Registration

It is important to understand the provisions in the Act that compel a data user to register and give the subject access to his own data.

The Data Protection Registrar keeps a public record of all individuals and organisations which hold personal data. It also states the type of data and also what it is used for. This record is available in most public libraries and also on the Registrar's website.

Every Data User who holds Personal Data must be registered unless exempt. The Registrar enters the following information given to her onto the Data Protection Register:

- Personal Data which the Data User holds.
- Purposes for which the data is used.
- Sources from which the data comes from.
- People/organisations to whom the data will be disclosed.
- Any places overseas where the data is to be transferred.

There is a duty on Data Users to ensure that the Register entries relating to the Personal Data they hold is correct and up to date.

Therefore whenever a viewer wants to find out what information gathering activities a data User is doing the first port of call must be this register. It states what information is being gathered. However the register only contains general information. How can an individual find out what information is held about him?

Subject Access

It no use knowing what the act says and the safeguards it gives individuals if those individual s have no way of knowing whether it is being complied with. This is where the right of subject access is important.

Individuals can, by making a written request to any Data User, get a copy of any Personal Data held about them. They can also ask for it to be corrected or deleted. A reply to such a request must be made within 40 days.

The request has to be made in writing giving sufficient details of the company to identify the individual. A fee of £10 is payable.

This is a very powerful tool to know exactly what information a company has got. Once a copy is received then it can be seen whether the act is being complied with and in particular whether the principles are being followed. If they are not a complaint to the registrar should be made.

Enforcement

If a data holder has breached any of the provisions of the act, the may face legal action from one of three sources.

A) Registrar

She is responsible for enforcing the Act. She has a duty to consider complaints and investigate. She has wide ranging powers to demand compliance with the act. It is she who would begin any criminal proceedings.

B) The Courts

The Data Protection Act creates 15 new criminal offences. These include holding unregistered Personal Data, making a disclosure to a person not registered and holding Personal Data for purposes not described in the Register.

Sanctions include a fine of up to £5,000 and costs in the Magistrates Court and an unlimited fine in the higher courts. There is no power of arrest or imprisonment.

C) The Subject of Data Collection: You

Individuals can claim compensation from the Data User for money lost or distress suffered because of inadequate security by the Data User if:

- Information held about them is inaccurate.
- The Data User has lost data.
- Data has been disclosed to someone not mentioned in the Register.
- Data has been destroyed without the authorisation of the Data User.

The Data Subject can also get a court order to correct or erase inaccurate data, or erase unauthorised access if this is likely to happen again.

These remedies are in addition to rights given by the general law e.g. Defamation, Consumer Credit Act 1974.

Conclusion

The Data Protection Act is an extremely important piece of legislation which gives rights and imposes obligations on Data Subjects and Data Users respectively. Used effectively it can be a powerful tool against a TV companies gathering information.

The Data Protection Act 1998

The Data protection Act 1998 comes into force on the 1st March 2000. The Act creates radical change to the UK's data protection regime. It places more obligations on the data users and it strengthens the rights of data subjects. Chief amongst these changes, which will allow people to fight back against the information excesses of interactive TV, are as follows:

- **Manual Files:** The Act will apply to certain manual files. To be covered, the particular data held on a manual file has to be part of a set of information which is:

"…structured by reference to individuals or by reference to criteria relating to individuals in such a way that specific information in relation to an individual is readily accessible."

(Section 1(1) 1998 Act)

In essence this means that where as previously data protection only covered data which was automatically processed, now it will cover any set of organised files. This means that whereas now TV companies can avoid the 1984 act by keeping the information they gather in manual files, they will have to disclose the contents of these files too when the 98 Act comes into force. This means that complainants and those wishing to know what information TV companies have on them will have access to much more data than before.

- **Direct Marketing:** This is a very important weapon in the struggle against abuse of personal data collected by TV companies. It may be they sell it to organisations who will use the information for the purpose of marketing. Or indeed they may use the information themselves to conduct direct marketing. Here section 11 of the Act requires closer examination :

"11 (1) An individual is entitled at any time by notice in writing ….to require the data controller…to cease or not to begin processing for the purpose of direct marketing personal data in respect of which he is the data subject. (2)… (3) In this section direct marketing means the communication (by whatever means) of any advertising or marketing material which is directed to particular individuals"

Thus in my view an individual who is the subject of direct marketing either through mailshots or through direct advertising can, using this section, ask the TV company to stop using his personal data for this purpose. Under Section 11(2) a court could order the company to take any steps if it failed to comply. Note the definition of direct marketing uses the words "by any means". Thus once the Act comes into force individuals will have a right to stop TV companies from processing their data in an important way.

- **Subject Access:** The Act strengthens individuals' rights to receive a copy of their data. These will not only cover computer file but also manual records, as discussed above. The individual must be told who the sources and the recipients of the data are.
- **Justification:** For the first time TV companies will have to justify why they are holding personal data. This must be done in relation to Schedule 2 of the new act. Whilst they may not have difficulty doing this e.g. it is done by consent or to fulfil a contract, it shows that mere holding the data is not enough.
- **Sensitive Data:** Any TV company holding data about categories such as race and health will have to show more justification and also what security measures they operate. Furthermore they will also have to obtain the explicit consent of the individual to holding such data.

It is clear that the data protection Act 1984 and the new data Protection Act 1998 do place a lot of responsibilities on companies who gather personal data using interactive TV. Those who want to ensure that these companies do not abuse their power should learn the provisions of the above act and exercise their rights under them. If they do this they will be able to prevent the harm of abuse of personal data which is so very possible with such a powerful tool as interactive TV.

Bibliography

2001: The Shape of TV to Come, Maggie Brown, *Daily Telegraph*

A Fly on the Virtual Wall; Cybercommunities Observed, Myra Stark, *Digitrends* – www.digitrends.net

A Piece of the Interaction, *Marketing Week,* 27 May 1994

Amazon Internet Feature Too Close To Home for Some, Jane Martinson, *Guardian,* 31 August 1999, London

Amazon website – www.amazon.com

American Academy of Pediatrics, 1999, Policy Statement: Media Education (RE9911), *Pediatrics,* Volume 104, Number 2

Andromedia website – www.andromedia.com

As Polularity Rises, Competition Thickens for The Interactive Television Market, Frost & Sullivan, PR Newswire

Barney and Friends Teach Interface Design by Margaret Quan, *TechWeb EE Times,* 31 May, 1999 – www.techweb.com/se/directlink.cgi?EET19990531S0049

Behavioural Aspects of Marketing, Keith C. Williams, Butterworth-Heinemann, Oxford, 1981

Beyond Branding to Bonding, Bernadette Tracy, Digitrends – www.digitrends.net

Big Brother Inside Boycott Intel website – www.bigbrotherinside.com

Bowling Alone: America's Declining Social Capital, Robert Putnam, *Journal of Democracy,* 6:1, January 1995

Brand Games website – www.brandgames.com

Cable: From Passive to Active, Adrian Chamberlain, address to FT Conference 4, March 1999 – reprinted on www.cwcom.co.uk

Center for Media and Democracy – www.prwatch.org

Digital TV Report, Liz Camps, www.digitaltvreport.com, 1998

Eh-oh! What is Bill Gates doing to our Tubbies? Jim McClellan, *Observer,* 31 January 1999

Europe and U.S. Are Still at Odds Over Privacy, Edmund L. Andrews, *New York Times,* 27 May 1999

Family Power '99™, 25-26 October, 1999, conference website – www.kidpowerx.com

FTC Finds No Need for Laws Protecting Online Privacy, Jeri Clausing, *New York Times,* 13 July 1999

George Washington, first draft of inaugural speech 1789, missing page reprinted in *Daily Telegraph,* 30 May, 1996, London

Get A Life! The Little Red Book of the White Dot Anti-television Campaign, David Burke and Jean Lotus, Bloomsbury, London, 1998

Heroic Online Branding: Exploring the Current and Future State of Interactive Marketing for the Entertainment industry and Its Consumer Brand Partners,

Elaine Palmer, *Digitrends* – www.digitrends.net

Inside the Mind of the Consumer, Emily Booth, *Direct Marketing*, 3 June 1999

Interactive Television: When's the Show Start? Joe Flower, *New Scientist*, March 1995, London

Interactive TV Advertising: Revolutionising the Advertising Industry, 15-16 July 1999, conference website – www.access-conf.com

Interactive TV Today, November 10 1999 Issue 2.45, www.itvt.com

International Firmas Smile on Wink's Technology, Jim Davis, CNET News.com, 6 July 1999

InTouch TV website – www.intouch.com

Kellogg's Clubhouse website – www.kelloggs.com/club/index.html

Key Marketing Issues in Attracting the Interactive User, Andrew Curry, ITV '96, http://www.ed.ac.uk/~rcss/iTV

Kid Power '99™, 26-27 April, 1999, conference website – www.kidpowerx.com

Koplar Interactive Systems International website – www.k-isi.com

Limits to the Imagination: Marketing & Children's Culture, Stephen Kline, published in *Lifestyle Shopping: The Subject of Consumption*, Rob Shields editor Routledge, New York, 1992

Marketing and Information Technology, John O'Connor and Eamonn Galvin, Pitman Publishing, London, 1997

Microsoft website – www.microsoft.com

Milia Media Mart, Steve Shipside, *Guardian*, 18 February, 1999

Net Companies Look Offline for Consumer Data, Bob Tedeschi, *New York Times*, 21 June 1999

No Place to Hide, Max Daly, *Big Issue*, 16 August 1999

Online Reputation & Public Relations Management, 27-28 July 1999, conference website – www.iqpc.com

Propaganda, Edward Bernays, Horace and Liverright, New York, 1928

Reading the Mind of the Market, Jennifer Schenker, *Time*, 2 August, 1999

Reuters, Privacy Group See Danger in a Merger, *New York Times*, 22 June 1999

Ruel.Net website – www.ruel.net

Rules on Children's Privacy Leave Web Sites Wondering, Pamela Mendels, *New York Times*, 22 April 1999

Television's Tribal Gatherings, David Wood and Peter Keighron, *Broadcast Magazine*, 30 April 1999, London

The Business of Children's Entertainment, Norma Odom Pecora, Guildford Press, New York, 1998

The Children Who Will Be Tomorrow's TV Citizens, Steve Morrison, *Guardian*, 27 September, 1999

The Palace website – www.thepalace.com

The Promise of One to One (A Love Story), Chip Bayers, *Wired*, May 1998

The Responsive Chord, Tony Schwartz, Anchor Press, Garden City, NJ, 1974

Tivo Inc. website – www.tivo.com

Toddlers Eat Less But Get Fatter on a Diet of TV, *The Independent,* 14 October, 1999

Toxic Sludge is Good for You, John Stauber and Sheldon Rapmton, Common Courage Press, Maine, 1995

Two Way TV website – www.twowaytv.com

Use Technology to Raise Smarter, Happier Kids: Behold the Toys of Tomorrow, David Shenk, *Atlantic*, 7 January 1999

We Have Your DNA, *PR Watch* Vol.4, No1 / First Quarter 1997

WebTV is Watching You, Karen Bannan, Inter@ctive Week Online – www.zdnews.com

Young People New Media, Sonia Livingstone, London School of Economics and Political Science, 1999

Acknowledgements

Jean Lotus started all this by founding White Dot. She also found and investigated Population Communications International. Deirdre Devers wrote the Fun chapter and contributed research throughout. She and Simon Davies of Privacy International advised on all aspects of writing and organising. The Big Brother Awards, run by Davies, are a needed inspiration to anyone concerned about privacy. With good humour, Pete Pavement nudged this book to completion, stronger and more ambitious than it could have been without him. Erica Smith offered me a chance to win a basket of groceries. Paul Stones organised White Dot's Zocalo when I was unavailable. I am belatedly grateful to Mick Butler for waking up early to stand in the cold outside Westminster Abbey holding a banner.

The following people have donated their knowledge of computer programming to this book and its website: Luke Boucher, Rick Belli, Caspar Hoskins and Richard Parry.

I am grateful to the following people for sharing their professional knowledge: Caspar Bowden of the Foundation for Information Policy Research, Sheldon Rampton and John Stauber of the Center for Media & Democracy, Jeff Chester of the Center for Media Education, Sonia Livingstone of LSE, Greg Philo of the University of Glasgow Media Unit, Andrew Curry now of the Henley Centre for Forecasting, Emily Booth of Direct Marketing, Ibrahim Hasan of Bradford Council, journalist Mike Kingston, Simon Trewin of Sheil Land, Ivan Stang of the Subgenius Foundation.

The professionals who contributed most were, of course, the television executives and marketing consultants I interviewed, all of whom were friendly and generous with their time.

I wish to thank friends for their encouragement, their interest in this project and for luring me away from it whenever possible with coffee or beer. I am grateful to my wife Karen, who gave up a lot this year to ensure that I had time to work, and a life away from it. She had help from my daughter Emily, who arranged visits to the playground. This book is dedicated to my mom, who told me as a child:"They only advertise things on TV if they're no good." and my dad who, a couple of years later, turned to me and demanded: "Why am I watching this stuff? It's got me all worked up for nothing! I'm just wasting my time!" It was a scary moment for both of us.